Glacier Bay

D0194486

A Guide to
Glacier Bay National Park
And Preserve, Alaska

Produced by the
Division of Publications
National Park Service

U.S. Department of the Interior
Washington, D.C. 1983

Using This Handbook
The major attractions at Glacier Bay National Park
and Preserve are the bay and its tidewater glaciers;
the whales and other wildlife of land, sea, and air;
the abrupt and massive Fairweather Range; and the
vast unspoiled outer coast. Part 1 of this handbook
briefly introduces the park and its history; Part 2
takes a close look at the dynamics of tidewater
glaciers and the natural history of both bay and
landscape; and Part 3 presents concise travel guide
and reference materials.

National Park Handbooks, compact introductions to
the great natural and historic places administered by
the National Park Service, are published to support
the National Park Service's management programs
at the parks and to promote understanding and
enjoyment of the parks. Each is intended to be
informative reading and a useful guide before,
during, and after a park visit. More than 100 titles
are in print. This is Handbook 123.

Library of Congress Cataloging in Publication Data
Main entry under title:
Glacier Bay: a guide to Glacier Bay National
Park and Preserve, Alaska.
(National park handbook; 123)
Bibliography: p.   Includes index.
Supt. of Docs. no.: I 29.9/5:123
1. Glacier Bay National Park and Preserve
(Alaska)—Guide-books. I. United States. National
Park Service. Division of Publications. II. Series:
Handbook (United States. National Park Service.
Division of Publications); 123.
F912.G5G57   1983   917.98′2   83-600088
ISBN 0-912627-17-4

Welcome to Glacier Bay

The Gem of Alaska's Inside Passage

A hiker packs through a lush meadow high above Tidal Inlet, about halfway up Glacier Bay. Since John Muir's day, the bay has attracted thousands of travelers, most of them waterborne. Part 1 of this handbook recounts the Glacier Bay travel tradition, from early explorations and scientific expeditions to the first tourists on steamships. Great cruise ships today ply the bay, introducing its wonders to travelers. Others come by air and by private water craft.

Pages 4 5: The serene bay surface may burst open to emit a 35-ton acrobatic humpback whale, or a towering wall of glacier ice may calve off stupendous icebergs. The unexpected pleasures of Glacier Bay and Southeast Alaska are nearly limitless.

Alaska's Glacier Bay confronts us with a mad jumble of paradoxes. Attempts to describe it juxtapose references to thunderous booming of ice and overwhelming silence. The landscape rests both brashly new and bedrock old, at once eternal and transitory, everlasting and ephemeral. The ice sheets lock up climatic history while rewriting today's topography. The crushing magnitude contrasts with the uncanny finesse of staged plant recovery. It is as though two worlds were unrolling like the ends of a scroll—ice receding and vegetation advancing. Might there not be a seam between these two worlds, one wonders, some extra-dimensional passage? No. Both are but landscapes and timescapes of our own one world.

John Muir came here in 1879 pursuing the reality of what he had earlier tracked as a mere ghost throughout California's High Sierra. He had trekked the California highcountry to find telltale etchings of massive glaciation, wishing to demonstrate the then novel and religiously disruptive glaciation theories of Swiss scientist Louis Agassiz. In Glacier Bay country, just below the shoulder of Alaska's south-reaching coastal arm, Muir trekked the real thing in action. He contemplated landscapes newly emerged from the Little Ice Age, a geologically recent winter's night that had lasted some ten centuries. Muir knew: At Glacier Bay you can get lost both in space and in time.

Muir's letters to the San Francisco *Bulletin* newspaper attracted Eliza Ruhamah Scidmore to Glacier Bay. "Steaming slowly up the inlet, the bold, cliff-like front of the glacier grew in height as we approached it," she wrote on her second trip in 1885, "and there was a sense of awe as the ship drew near enough for us to hear the strange, continual rumbling of the subterranean or subglacial waters, and see the avalanches of ice that, breaking from the front, rushed down into the sea with tremendous

crashes and roars." Despite the whales, despite the seals, despite the stupendous coastal mountain scenery, it is first and foremost the stark drama of tidewater glaciers that makes Glacier Bay the gem of southeastern Alaska's protected coastal sea lane known as the Inside Passage. "Words and dry figures can give one little idea of this glacial torrent," Scidmore wrote, " . . . the beauty of the fantastic ice front, shimmering with all the prismatic hues, is beyond imagery or description." Her first glimpse of Muir Glacier had reduced her to silence. Today, thousands of people visit Glacier Bay each summer. Most come by cruise ship, others fly into nearby Gustavus, or directly to the park in charter aircraft. The park's mountains, the Fairweather and St. Elias Ranges, are perhaps the world's most spectacularly glaciated mountains. The bay itself is home to seals, porpoises, and whales. The mountainous shores are dotted with birdlife, with black bears and brown/grizzly bears, and with mountain goats.

Recorded history as we generally credit it had begun for the Glacier Bay area nearly 150 years before Muir's coming. The log of the Russian packet boat *St. Paul*, commanded by Alexis Tchirikov, records for July 15, 1741: "This must be America, judging by the latitude and longitude." Tchirikov had sighted the Fairweather Range. The next day his compatriot Vitus Bering sighted land north of here and named Mt. St. Elias. Bering's name survives as a sea, a strait, and as a former land bridge between Russia and what is now Alaska. Tchirikov's log book survived the voyage; Tchirikov did not.

Actually, the Fairweather—a misnomer!—Range was not named until 1778, when James Cook, commanding His Majesty's sloop, *Resolution*, sailed into the area. For the next several years, assorted Russians and Aleuts lured by sea otters visited, but no records survive. Then in 1786 Frenchman Jean Francois de Galaup, comte de Lapérouse, put into what is now Lituya Bay. Tlingit Indian legend records Lapérouse's visit, calling him Yealth. He managed to "purchase" Cenotaph Island from one Tlingit chief, leaving a medallion and records to that effect stashed in rocks there; these either remain undiscovered or were destroyed by later Russian or other visitors. He spent 27 days in Lituya Bay, and his log book describes in detail both Tlingits and the surrounding gigantic wilderness. Not least, he describes a calving berg: "A fragment of ice, which fell into the water near half a mile off, occasioned such a swell along the shore, that my boat was upset, and thrown to some distance on the border of the glacier. This accident was soon repaired, and we returned on board. . . ." Mt. La Perouse and the magnificent La Perouse Glacier on the park's outer coast inscribe this Frenchman's name here.

By the time of Lapérouse and Cook, explorers were plying the American Northwest Coast fueled by a rich mixture of greed and geographic misinformation. They sought the mythic Northwest Passage, that supposed navigable route across North America to a lucrative China trade. Imagine then their disappointment to confront staggering glacial blockades walling off progress inland so immediately after they quit the open Pacific.

The number of discrete tidewater glaciers has increased significantly since Capt. George Vancouver, who had been a midshipman on Cook's ship, spied what would become Glacier Bay from Icy Strait on his own expedition in 1794. Simply put, the entire bay was then one mighty ice sheet almost to its mouth.

If Eliza Scidmore was one of Glacier Bay's first tourists, she was soon succeeded not by more tourists but by glaciologists and plant ecologists. Spectacles of nature abound throughout most of Alaska, but in Glacier Bay you can still step right off the Little Ice Age and walk across nearly two centuries of plant succession, seeing how ice-scoured land recovers by stages to mature coastal forest. Glacier Bay offered glaciologists and plant ecologists a compact natural laboratory of time and space too good to pass up. "Discovered" in 1879, prominent by 1884, world famous by 1886, the Muir Glacier that Scidmore saw would next be unattainable by tourists. An earthquake rocked the Alaskan coast at 12:20 p.m. on September 10, 1899. Within hours, Glacier Bay was a mass of impenetrable floating ice. The glacier's terminus was devastated by the quake and went into rapid retreat. For the next few years ships could generally get within only 8 kilometers (5 miles) of the Muir Ice front. This cataclysmic change marked the end of the era of description for Glacier Bay. The era of explanation then began, and continues today, as Ruth Kirk testifies in Part 2 of this handbook.

Several Glacier Bay facts amply demonstrate the rapid, massive changes here: Tchirikov could not have entered Glacier Bay in 1741 because it was a vast ice sheet. Captain Vancouver found Icy Strait much choked with ice in 1794, and Glacier Bay was a mere dent in the shoreline then. Yet by 1879 John Muir found that the sometimes 1,200-meter- (4,000-foot) thick mantle of ice had retreated 77 kilometers (48 miles) up the bay. By 1916 the Grand Pacific Glacier stood 105 kilometers (65 miles) from the mouth of Glacier Bay. This rapid pace of glacial retreat is known nowhere else in the world. This central fact, plus its exemplification of plant succession, its great natural beauty, and its value to marine mammals and other wildlife, inspired the move to protect Glacier Bay.

The Ecological Society of America, with the impetus of William S. Cooper who had studied the plant succession and relict forests, in 1923 recommended that a national monument be established at Glacier Bay. Five reasons were enumerated: the tidewater glaciers; other scientific features, including ancient forest remnants; the coastal forests; the historical associations since Vancouver's time; and the relative accessibility to travel, compared with other tidewater glacier areas. The Society recommended a national monument because such areas could be established by Presidential proclamation, whereas national parks could be created only by Congress. In 1924, President Calvin Coolidge ordered the temporary withdrawal of one million hectares (2.5 million acres), and in 1925 he proclaimed the Glacier Bay National Monument. All seemed well.

Local agitation for opening the area to mining followed, however, and in 1936 a bill to do just this was quickly approved by Congress two days before its adjournment for the Democratic National Convention. President Franklin Delano Roosevelt signed it three days later. Conservationists who had worked two years for the monument's establishment with mining excluded were shocked.

With support from the U.S. Department of Agriculture, the monument boundary was enlarged significantly in 1939. Again because of local pressure

Pages 16-17: *The Fair-weather Range's Mount Bertha wears soft hues of morning light. The Fair-weathers rise abruptly from tidewater, walling the bay's western shore.*

Pages 18-19: *A big hump-back whale outweighs eight African elephants. Curious, friendly, and playful, this mysteriously intelligent and talkative whale is an endangered species.*

however, the boundary was reduced somewhat in 1955. Another large addition to the monument was made in 1978. In 1980, Congress redesignated the area Glacier Bay National Park and Preserve. The national park now includes some 1.3 million hectares (3.2 million acres) and the national preserve some 23,000 hectares (57,000 acres). The national park portion is closed to mining, of course, and much of it is further protected as part of the National Wilderness Preservation System. These management distinctions are explained in Part 3 of this handbook.

The 1930s mining flap unwittingly centered about an indefatigable prospector named Joe Ibach. He put ashore at Ptarmigan Creek, northwest of Reid Glacier, in the early summer of 1925. Nearby Ibach hit gold-bearing veins and staked them, registering them later that summer. So began a three-decade association with Reid Inlet for Joe and his wife, Muz, just as, on the other side of the continent, the fight for establishing the monument was just grinding toward resolution.

The Ibachs' gold operations, in association first with Capt. Tom Smith and later with novelist Rex Beach, never amounted to anything. One season's yield was enough to cover the smelting work in Juneau, but not the freight, for which the smelter billed Ibach and Smith! The next year was more profitable. After all was said and done, Joe and Muz netted $13 and Smith netted $13. At that, the latter threw in his pick and sledge. Beach never realized anything from mining here.

The cabin that still stands at the entrance to Reid Inlet was built by the Ibachs about 1940 and Muz soon put in the vegetable garden with dirt hauled in ore sacks from Lemesurier Island. Three spruces, also imports, were planted there far ahead of their ecological time, since the Reid Glacier was then less than 5 kilometers (3 miles) away. Captain Smith recounts that Joe and Muz had agreed that if one of the couple died while they were in the wilds together, the other would die right away. "I think I would feel the same way," Smith reflected, "if I had lived out there all that time with a wife." The Ibachs' last year together at Reid Inlet was 1956. Muz died in Juneau's St. Ann's Hospital in 1959. Joe died in 1960, still planning to visit Reid Inlet. The morning after planning his return, Joe shot himself. At the bottom of his will, written on brown wrapping paper, Joe had added: "There's a time to live and a time to die. This is the time." The unconscious ambiguity somehow sits well in this terrain of paradoxes.

Of all Glacier Bay's extremely few residents since Indian days, perhaps only Joe and Muz Ibach and Jim Huscroft stand out. Huscroft lived alone on Cenotaph Island in Lituya Bay from 1915 or 1917 to 1939, when he died there, still alone. He was the only outer coast resident for a 240-kilometer (150-mile) stretch. Once a year he went to Juneau for supplies and to pick up the past year's stack of newspapers, saved for him at the Elks Club. Back home on the island, he read one paper a day, a year late, never cheating by reading ahead one day. Huscroft's biggest yearly event was Christmas dinner. He sat down to it alone with the choice of 14 kinds of homemade pie!

There must be profound satisfaction in venturing, as Eliza Scidmore did, to such an area as Glacier Bay so early in its tourist history. Indeed, after describing the Muir ice front and "the crack of the rending ice, the crash of the falling fragments" with their steady undertone like the boom of Yosemite Falls, Scidmore adds this note: "There was something, too, in the consciousness that so few had ever gazed upon the scene before us, and there were neither guides nor guide books to tell us which way to go, and what emotions to feel." Those words appear, paradoxically, in her illustrated guidebook, *Journeys in Alaska*, issued the very next summer. We hope this Glacier Bay handbook serves you as well as hers served a generation of Alaskan travelers.

Of Time and Ice

Tidewater Glaciers

Ice research vessel Growler *rests in Johns Hopkins Inlet. Author Ruth Kirk traveled aboard with glaciologists for one of her many Glacier Bay trips. In Part 2 of this handbook she recounts her travels, the dynamics of tidewater glaciers, and the park's natural history. Depth readings made aboard* Growler *and* Bergy-bit—*hanging astern on davits—are interpreted for you by the illustration on pages 46 and 47.*

Pages 22-23: Pan ice simmers golden in low sun on Johns Hopkins Inlet.

In a small way, I once touched time. It was July and my husband, Louis, and I were camped in Reid Inlet, an exquisite fjord fingering off Glacier Bay's main, upper waterway. Our tent was pitched near a 1940s gold miner's shack, which that summer was serving as headquarters for park ranger Ole Wik and his wife, Manya. Rock peaks and ridges walled our horizon. At the inlet's head a glacier tongue calved icebergs directly into saltwater. From basketball to Detroit limousine size, these ice chunks rode the currents and stranded ashore on each outgoing tide, making the beach a sculpture garden. Manya lugged small stranded bergs home in pails hung from a shoulder yoke. The ice turned a pit dug in the coarse upper beach gravel into an icebox.

One evening, the Wiks and Louis and I decided to make ice cream in an old hand-crank freezer. Out from the pit came fresh eggs, which Manya mixed with powdered milk dissolved in creek water and sweetened with honey. Ole and Louis chipped salvaged bergs and packed the ice fragments into the freezer. We turned the crank till it would turn no more and then spooned out the ice cream.

Icebergs floated on the tide just offshore. We sat reveling in the 11 p.m. sunset and feasting on the ice cream. A cormorant, its sleek body and upright neck a dark silhouette against the water's pink tint, rode one berg. New bergs sporadically broke from the glacier, their birthing thunder a syncopation for the evening's hush. Ole mused aloud on our having used the iceberg's fossilized cold to freeze the ice cream. For the ice it concluded unknown decades of an existence begun as fluffy snow and then compressed to ice, owing to the sheer weight of snow accumulating above it.

By the Grand Pacific Glacier: Reid Inlet ice cream comes to mind now, four Julys later, as I cook breakfast aboard *R.V. Growler*, a U.S. Geological Survey ice research boat. Oatmeal bubbles on the galley's oil range as I set out the corn muffins I've baked. The big galley table is at once workbench, library desk, and center for food preparation, eating, and socializing.

Five of us are aboard. In charge is glaciologist Austin Post—tall, strong, with a grizzled beard that hangs to his chest and gentle eyes that laugh. His assistants, college-age, capable, enthusiastic, are David Janka, Emily Chase, and Austin's son Charles Post. My role is as observer and photographer.

For two hours we've been taking depth readings in front of Tarr Inlet's Grand Pacific Glacier. Its ice, along with that of the Margerie Glacier, blocks the extreme upper end of Glacier Bay. Data recorded by *Growler's* electronic sounder will make it possible to chart the bottom contours here. The contours will help in understanding tidewater ice, which responds to various factors aside from climate. Why, for example, is the Grand Pacific Glacier advancing, while just to the east, the Muir Glacier has been rapidly retreating for a century? What accounts for such diverse behavior in the same area?

Glacier ice today whitens a tenth of the world's land surface, as much as is now farmed. A few thousand years ago glaciers covered triple this area, as they someday surely will again. Boston's Bunker Hill is a drumlin left behind by glacier ice. Erratic boulders dot Manhattan's Central Park, transported from Canada by glacier ice. Duck hunters in Minnesota set decoys on pothole lakes formed by melting ice remnants. Plains farmers grow wheat in loess, windblown glacial sediment. French vineyards are also in loess. Drink French wine and you toast the Ice Age. Yet despite the magnitude and recurrence of glaciers, knowledge of them is little more than well begun. Glacier Bay is one of the widely recognized field laboratories for glaciology.

Growler is in Glacier Bay as part of a continuing study of tidewater ice. Austin Post can visualize these ice tongues and how they behave. For 20 years he has been making aerial photographs of glaciers from the Andes to the Aleutians and painstakingly mapping their changes. Austin does not merely rejoice to know that the world is not only blue and green but also white. He *prefers* the white. When I came aboard *Growler*, he asked me about the weather in Seattle. "Sunny and hot," I said. "That's awfully hard on the ice," Austin muttered in reply.

At the wheel Austin is now maneuvering *Growler* through floating icebergs. They aren't packed solid this morning and we can work to within one-third kilometer (1,000 feet) of the Grand Pacific's ice face. We won't go closer because of danger from falling ice, but we'll send a small, radio-controlled skiff to bump against the glacier snout and read the water depth there. The glacier front is not floating. It rests on a rubble ridge of its own making. Emily, Dave, and Chuck are with Austin in the wheelhouse, correlating *Growler's* precise position with the depth-sounder record and with Polaroid pictures of the radar scope. I can be spared to cook, but everyone else is needed for the readings. It's 0800 now. We've been underway since 0630 and will soon cut the engine to drift with the pack ice and eat breakfast.

A moment ago we were swept off course by a melt torrent draining from under the glacier. No depth reading registered until we worked free of its flow, because the stream disgorges so much suspended mineral material that the signal from our depth sounder dispersed instead of striking bottom and bouncing back. Even the water surface is gray with glacial flour, bedrock ground to powder by the pressure of moving ice. Away from the ice front the gray becomes turquoise as the silt mutes but no longer dominates the clear, deep blue of open water. Often distinct color bands persist, their moiré pattern maintained by the water's different temperatures and salinities. Such banding may reach all the way to Icy Strait, 70 kilometers (43 miles) from the nearest tidewater glaciers. We terrestrials think of seawater as homogeneous. It's not.

Nor is a glacier just a mass of frozen water. It is ice, plus flowing water, plus a vast amount of rock debris scoured, rasped, and plucked from the mountains where glaciers are born and from the valley walls and bottoms they inch across en route downslope. In the color banding of a fjord's water surface you witness the sedimentation process that in time fills in enormous submarine troughs and turns waterways into valleys with freshwater streams and wildflowers.

Out *Growler's* porthole the far side of the Margerie Glacier is so blackened with rubble that it looks like rock. Only a melt sheen identifies it from this distance as glacier ice. Directly ahead of us, moraines of rock debris streak the length of the Grand Pacific Glacier like ribbons. At the sides of the ice face they show as tilted layers dipping into the water. Moraines form as rock tumbles and slides from steepened slopes onto the glacier surface, there to ride the ice and eventually break free as part of an iceberg, or to be released by melt. Moraines are among the legacies of glaciation. They form abrupt ridges of loose rock, gravel, and sand often several-score meters high and extending for long distances. Though in time moraines may become upholstered with plants, their origin remains easily recognizable.

When mineral debris is dropped directly beneath a glacier it may form hills and short ridges known as kames and drumlins, or, if deposited by a subglacial stream, as eskers. Last evening we anchored *Growler* a half-hour's run south of the Margerie ice front, then hiked up a side drainage and sat at dusk watching a loon paddle across a small lake impounded by an esker. Slices of time seemed separated from eternity's flow and laid before us. We had walked through a carpet of dryas plants shaggy with seedheads. Dryas can pioneer poor soil and so can quickly form a green aftermath of glacier ice. We had hoped to find glacio-marine clay—lumps dropped, usually, from floating icebergs—remnants from millennia ago when seawater covered where we sat watching the loon.

Floating bergs, the white peaks, and the processes of mineral transport and deposit, have all repeatedly characterized the Glacier Bay scene. Until recently, geologists believed that the last million years had brought four major ice ages. Now they see these as composite glacier advances, retreats, and re-advances. The number of such pulses was closer to 40 than to four, with one series often hard to discern from another.

Expanding glaciers clear virtually everything movable from their paths, so nothing more than traces of early glaciations are likely to remain. One such trace lies along the outer coast of Glacier Bay National Park. Marine tillite, glacial debris deposited in seawater, is there interbedded with layers of siltstone and sandstone for a total thickness of nearly 2,000 meters (6,500 feet). The ancient tillite formed by the same mineral dumping process I've been

Researchers ready depth-recording instruments inside Bergy-bit's *covered hull (top). Glaciologist Austin Post (middle) plots bathymetric contours aboard* Growler. Bergy-bit's *chart (bottom) shows the Gilman Glacier ice front. On the author's trip aboard* Growler, Bergy-bit *charted an underwater canyon at the Johns Hopkins Glacier ice front.*

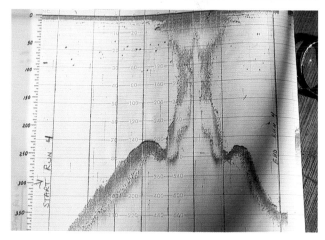

Post-Glacial Land Features

Retreating glaciers leave behind characteristic land features, some shaped by the ice, others by meltwater. In your travelogue, impress your friends with the technical term: glacio-geomorphological features.

❶Eskers form as a stream tunnel beneath a glacier fills in with rubble. Eskers look like inverted streams winding snake-like across today's landscape.

Moraines form in various ways. ❷Lateral moraines form where the sides of a glacier shove up mounds or ridges. ❸End moraines, glacial dumps at the snout of retreating ice, trend perpendicular to its flow. Ground

moraines are deposited under moving ice. ❹The dark stripes on Casement Glacier (below) are medial moraines. They were once the lateral moraines of the tributary glaciers squeezed together to form this glacier.

❺Outwash plains are meltwater features. The broad, flat riverbed and braided stream are typical. At times during the Ice Ages, the Mississippi River probably looked like this scene—on a grander scale.

❻Revegetation flourishes on higher ground. The outwash plain must fix its river channel before revegetation takes hold. Burdened by glacial silt, this streambed wanders over the valley, its changing course stymieing revegetation.

watching this morning. It comes complete with the rafted lumps such as we sought without success last evening—the sort that ride the icebergs I see out the porthole now.

Shells date the layered outer-coast sediments to about 15 million B.P. (before present). A park research biologist once told me he found a fossil beech leaf in the deposits. It must have been blown or washed seaward to settle in the ocean-bottom ooze. To have endured for 15 million years seems extraordinary; to be a beech leaf even more so. For that testifies to a scene far different than today's. Glacier ice was then juxtaposed with deciduous forest. Nowhere does such a situation exist today except in Chile where a relative of beech thrives close to ice.

For most of southeast Alaska, the signs of early glaciation are not deposition but erosion. Sharply sculpted high peaks are those plucked by ice. Lower, rounded contours were overridden. You can see this shift from craggy horn peaks to rounded and polished bedrock and so pinpoint the level of a former glacier. In lower Glacier Bay this line comes at about 1,300 meters (4,200 feet).

The period from about 30,000 to 10,000 B.P. brought the most recent worldwide glaciation, known in America as the Wisconsinan because the southern edge or terminus of a vast ice sheet sculpted much of that state's current topography. The Glacier Bay region—and practically all high latitudes and elevations—surrendered to ice during this time. Juneau lay beneath a white shroud 1,500 meters (5,000 feet) thick. At Cape Spencer on the park's outer coast the ice was still at least 900 meters (3,000 feet) thick, with its leading edge somewhere far beyond today's coastline.

Oddly, however, parts of the shore were not veneered by this ice. It may be they escaped because a geologic fault at the western base of the Fairweather mountains acted as a gutter and shunted off encroaching ice. Such faults are cracks in the Earth's surface. This one marks where the crustal plate comprising the Pacific Ocean floor abuts the crustal plate bearing the North American continent. California's famous San Andreas Fault is somewhat comparable. The Fairweather rift splits off land from Icy Point to Russell Fjord, north of Yakutat.

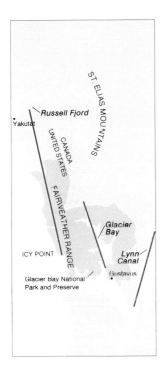

During the Wisconsinan advance the Glacier Bay region surrendered to a vast ice sheet, but part of the Outer Coast escaped this icy veneer. Scientists hypothesize that a geologic fault at the Fairweather Range's western base acted as a gutter, shunting off the encroaching ice. Faults show as red lines on this map.

Bedrock is out of alignment along opposite sides of the fault. In fact, whole provinces have slid northward as the oceanic plate collides with the continental plate and heaves up the mountains. Certain rock found at sea level south of Icy Point stands north of the Point at an elevation of more than 3,000 meters (10,000 feet). Less active faults underlie both Glacier Bay and Lynn Canal.

Above Tarr Inlet: It is afternoon and Dave and Emily and I have climbed onto the highest terrace of the slope above the Grand Pacific snout. Dave's altimeter shows our elevation as 269 meters (882 feet). A multi-decked cruise ship drifting among icebergs near the glacier face looks from here like an inconsequential dot. People on deck to watch bergs calve off must see the glacier front as immense. At 60 to 80 meters (200 to 260 feet) high and 6 kilometers (3.75 miles) across, it is.

From our vantage point you see how much more glacier there really is than shows from the water. Grand Pacific flows as an infinity of ice coming from far back in the mountains. Except for crevasses near the snout, its surface looks like a broad white highway, which is how several coastal Alaskan glaciers served Indians and prospectors traveling to and from the interior. Using Grand Pacific as a conduit, wolves and bears have extended their range onto Glacier Bay lands recently melted free of ice and beginning to host life again.

From where we sit it's easy to imagine Tarr Inlet stripped of today's ice, seeing instead either a continuation of today's waterway or a broad terrestrial valley bottom. As recently as the 1920s the Grand Pacific melted its way out of the United States and 2 kilometers (1.2 miles) into Canada. That gave Canada a potential site for her northwesternmost seaport. But by 1948 ice again moved forward as far as the border.

The Glacier Bay bedrock trough is tremendously deep, dropping to 550 meters (1,800 feet) near Gilbert Island. Muir Inlet reaches about 375 meters (1,200 feet), a considerable depth, yet the inlet completely filled with gravel following withdrawal of the Wisconsinan ice! This fill stood higher than present sea level, developing soil and a spruce-and-hemlock forest. Side valleys, dammed by the gravel, seem to have held lakes, because traces of glacial

The theory of worldwide glaciation, published in 1840, only slowly supplanted the Biblical flood in explaining contemporary landforms. Naturalist John Muir championed this glacial theory in the United States. Muir canoed into Glacier Bay with Tlingit paddlers in 1879 from Fort Wrangell to see first-hand the massive glacier now named for him.

outwash gravels cling 250 meters (820 feet) above today's saltwater shores, and lakebed sediments are still in place. Dr. Richard Goldthwait, emeritus professor at Ohio State University, believes that the fill in Muir, Wachusett, and Adams Inlets probably averaged 150 meters (500 feet) deep and 5 kilometers (3 miles) wide for a cumulative 80 kilometers (50 miles) of length. Except for mere whispers, this stupendous volume of gravel fill is now gone. Readvancing ice swept it into the Beartrack Cove area and on southward. The broad Gustavus flatlands are partly old Muir gravel fill.

Wisconsinan glaciers melted back perhaps 11,000 years ago and probably stayed back until about 3,500 years ago, when harsh climatic conditions again favored glacier expansion. Worldwide this Little Ice Age was not dramatic. At Glacier Bay, however, snowfall produced ice more than 1,000 meters (3,200 feet) thick and pushed the glaciers far forward. A tongue of ice once more filled the entire Glacier Bay fjord and bulged out into Icy Strait. This dammed Muir Valley and backed up an enormous lake there that drowned the forest.

About a thousand years after the glaciers' encroachment into the main Glacier Bay fjord, an ice tongue began to advance down Muir Valley. At the outlet it was blocked by the glacier already there. Unable to thrust farther forward, this new ice ponded and flowed back on itself, filling depressions along lower Muir Inlet to such depths that remnants still haven't melted today. They are popular destinations for hikers and give geologists a look at how melting glacier ice has produced much of today's northern-latitudes topography.

The ebullient, voluble, knowledgeable, and renowned John Muir was an early exponent of the continental glaciation theory in North America. He canoed north from Fort Wrangell in October 1879, coaxing his Tlingit Indian paddlers onward against their judgment. Fall struck them as a foolish season for venturing among icebergs. But for Muir ice was the reason for the journey. Aged 41, acclaimed champion of all nature, specifically fascinated by glaciation, Muir became the first Glacier Bay sightseer to write extensively and glowingly about the wonders of what now is the national park. His first trip was brief, but in the summer of 1880 and again in

Harry Fielding Reid first lugged his theodolite and plane table about Glacier Bay in 1890. So began the accurate plotting of ice positions that is critical to relating glacier behavior to climate change and other factors.

1890, Muir returned. By the time of his third trip, tourists were visiting Glacier Bay aboard side-wheel excursion steamers. Eliza Ruhamah Scidmore wrote in a *National Geographic* article of "stopping, backing, and going at half speed to avoid the floating ice all around ... [which] occasionally was ground and crunched up by the paddle wheels with a most uncomfortable sound."

The Muir Glacier—newly named for the famed naturalist—had scarcely begun its retreat at that time, though the ice filling Glacier Bay proper had drawn back 60 kilometers (37 miles) in the century since British Captain George Vancouver had noted its presence in 1794. This glacial unzipping is the fastest known anywhere, anytime.

Fortunately for the understanding of Glacier Bay's chronology, Harry Fielding Reid, a pioneering glaciologist, arrived here in 1890, about 30 years after the Glacier Bay unzipping had exposed the Muir Glacier for the first time. Through the summer of 1890 and again two summers later, Reid explored by rowboat and on foot, lugging a cumbersome theodolite and plane table for mapping glacier positions. "We once approached to within a quarter mile of the ice cliffs of Muir Glacier, which towered impressively above us," Reid wrote. "Suddenly a large berg broke off, followed immediately by a second, and then several arose from below. Great breakers which must have been 30 feet high, rushed forward, but fortunately subsided into an even swell before reaching us. The fragments of ice spread out with great rapidity and in a few minutes quite surrounded our boat."

The Grand Pacific Glacier was then fused with the Margerie, their joint terminus barely separated from the Johns Hopkins Glacier. Reid wrote that the continual calving of that great ice cliff, nearly 10 kilometers (6 miles) long, was "keeping the inlet well covered with floating ice and the air pulsating with the thunder of its fall."

No wonder the Tlingits thought John Muir reckless, though he gloried in the calving bergs' "awful roaring, tons of water streaming like hair down the sides, while they heave and plunge again and again before they settle in poise and sail away as blue-crystal islands, free at last. . . ." John Muir, too, had touched time.

Galloping, Calving, Advancing, Retreating

Mad wreckage of the retreating Muir Glacier ice front chokes adjacent waters. The glacier retreated about 5 kilometers (3 miles) between 1972 and 1982. It has retreated more than 25 kilometers (15 miles) in this century, at widely varying rates.

Johns Hopkins: All morning we have been charting in upper Johns Hopkins Inlet. The high peaks of the Fairweather Range thrust like white fangs above us. Beside us rise gray, bare, abrupt rock walls. We arrived here aboard *Growler* about 2100 last evening. Sunlight still flooded the upper walls but the water already stood in twilight, lending an eerie quality to this cathedral-like fjord. Eager to see whether the Tyeen Glacier had surged forward since last summer, we barely noticed, however. Austin, Dave, Emily, Charles, and I all crowded into the wheelhouse, with last year's aerial photograph on the chart table for comparison with what we hoped to see ahead, a glacier that galloped. Alas, no drama greeted us. The ice still hung near the top of the cliff, poised to surge, perhaps, but far from having done so.

Two hundred galloping glaciers are known in Alaska and northwestern Canada, some occasionally surging several kilometers in a single year. These extraordinary advances occur only on certain glaciers. No glaciers overlying granitic bedrock are given to surging. Many that do surge are associated with geologic faults, but not all. Water beneath the ice has been advanced as an explanation for galloping glaciers, but this can't be the whole answer.

A mountain glacier is usually rushing if it moves a meter or two (4 to 7 feet) a day. Deformation permits the ice to bend and slide around obstacles, and the enormous pressure against any such protrusion produces enough heat to melt a fraction of the glacier's undersurface. Lubricated by this minute film of meltwater, the ice jerks forward. That relieves the pressure and the melt-film refreezes. The process starts anew.

I once watched this happen where University of Washington researchers had dug a 25-meter (85-foot) tunnel to bedrock beneath the Blue Glacier in Washington's Olympic Mountains. Gauges imbedded in the tunnel walls measured the pressure the ice exerted against irregularities in its bed and the rate of its jerky flow over and around them. Dials dispassionately registered what was happening, but you could see it without them. A knob of bedrock might have ice pressed against it. Then a momentary wetness would darken the rock and an additional fraction of the knob would be engulfed. The process was silent and, but for the glaciologists' lights, would haven taken place in utter blackness.

Water beneath ice may not fully explain why some glaciers gallop, but meltwater—with land runoff— surely affects the rate at which Glacier Bay's glaciers perform their greatest scenic wonder: calving icebergs off their tidewater snouts.

The water works down through the ice and momentarily lifts the glacier off bedrock during brief periods of exceptional hydrostatic pressure. The lifting weakens the ice and accelerates collapse. Some feel that low tide may also step up calving. Ice in contact with saltwater melts more rapidly than ice exposed only to air, producing undercutting—and reduced support—at the high-tide line. Others find this erosive undercutting inconsequential to calving. Geological Survey monitoring establishes no relation between tide and calving rate.

Icebergs themselves are far from uniform. Those that look white hold myriad trapped air bubbles. Blue means denser ice. Greenish-black ice is from the bottom, or sole, of a glacier and such bergs may also be grooved where bedrock knobs have gouged the glacier. Morainal rubble stripes some icebergs with brown, or totally darkens them. Rocks ride atop bergs and plop into the water from their sides.

Stranding icebergs leave tracks as they half float, half drag along the beach. And they grind, squash, and rip seaweeds and mussels pioneering rocky shores. Floating bergs offer perches favored by bald eagles, cormorants, and gulls. For eagles the bergs seem to serve as movable vantage points for spotting opportunities to prey or scavenge. Cormorants often hold out their wings to dry while they ride. Most gulls just rest. Kittiwakes—gulls that come ashore only to nest—briefly ride Glacier Bay icebergs during their August transition from nesting colonies to life at sea. Guillemots and puffins never ride the bergs, perhaps because of difficulties landing on ice. Their legs, set far back and fine for swimming, are awkward out of water. Land birds, except for eagles, generally ignore icebergs.

As you kayak among bergs, paddling silently, you hear melt take its toll. Water drops and cascades. Air bubbles pop and ice cracks constantly as it adjusts to changing pressures and temperatures. Even with your eyes closed, you can tell icebergs are close. How high bergs float depends on their size and ice density and on the density of the water. Where runoff or rainwater floats atop saltwater, bergs sink lower than if freshwater is absent. The burden of rock and sediment in the ice sometimes weighs a small berg below the surface. A faint shadowy presence is all that gives it away.

Huge bergs, recognizable by distinctive shape or patterning, may last a week or more, though they split or turn over as reshaping melt affects balance. What had seemed a modest floating crag may, when rolling over, suddenly loom as an enormous hazard if you've paddled too near.

Studying a beached iceberg reveals its fabric and susceptibility to melt. Ice crystals that measure a centimeter (0.4 inches) or more across interlock as in a three-dimensional puzzle. Along such interfaces sun warmth and saltwater attack. Grasp a projection and wiggle it. You will hear a squeaking as the crystals rub one another along these junctions.

Last evening Dave stood near *Growler's* bow as we approached the upper end of Johns Hopkins Inlet. Net in hand, he scooped up icebergs for the refrigerator. We had run close to the Johns Hopkins and Gilman glacier faces to take bottom readings. For these, Austin used *Bergy-bit*, the little radio-controlled boat which amounts to a sleek hull fitted with a tight lid. Only its three-horsepower electric motor projects vulnerably. We placed one of *Growler's* depth sounders inside *Bergy-bit*.

Mid channel approaching the Johns Hopkins snout, *Growler* consistently recorded a water depth of 400 meters (1,300 feet) and a flat bottom, the sort of uniform contour expected of fine-grained sediments deposited in deep water. The water is so deep that there is no anchorage in this inlet. The bottom lies far beyond an anchor's reach even along the sidewalls. To our surprise, however, about one kilometer (1.5 miles) from the glacier face we measured water "only" 150 meters (500 feet) deep. The glacier is

Stumps are all that remain of ancient forests that flourished between the major ice advances. Some such silent park sentinels lived when Egypt's great pyramids were under construction.

Pages 40-41: Icebergs are not uniform. White ones hold myriad trapped air bubbles. Blue indicates denser ice. Greenish-black ice comes from the glacier bottom. Brown stripes denote morainal rubble. The sighings and creakings of an iceberg's slow demise are—with the percussive drip of meltwater—quite musical.

pushing a steep-sided submarine plug far out ahead of its front. Austin has found nothing like this elsewhere.

We sent *Bergy-bit* along the east side of the Johns Hopkins ice front, and the entire front of the Gilman Glacier, and then, barely before midnight, quit for dinner. For the past two hours I had supposed we would stop, so I kept spinach noodles hot on the stove, and they turned into a startling green goo. Rather than admit culinary defeat I topped the mass with Parmesan cheese and croutons and baked it. Camaraderie and hunger sufficed to prompt praise for my baked goo. By the time we finished dinner it was technically already morning.

We drifted all night. With the water too deep for anchorage, we had to depend on pack ice to hold us safely away from the fjord wall. We took turns standing watch, a long boat hook in hand for pushing off bergs that might cause trouble. At one point Emily roused Austin to start the engine and work free of encircling ice that brought with it an iceberg towering higher than *Growler's* rail.

Mostly it was a night of ethereal peace. There was no moon but the floating ice reflected enough light so that on watch you could make out closeby bergs and the seals circling us like dark phantoms. Occasionally a seal would signal the sudden end of its curiosity and slap the water with its hind flippers, then dive. Otherwise, the only sounds were a faint roar from distant waterfalls, the sporadic grinding of ice against *Growler's* hull, and once the splash of an iceberg rolling over.

This morning we resumed readings with *Bergy-bit*. I sit out of the way atop the wheelhouse while Dave controls the skiff with the radio transmitter and Emily watches with binoculars, telling him which way to turn so as to steer *Bergy* through leads in the ice pack. Falling ice strikes the little boat with a loud *clonk* and for a while *Bergy* vanishes from sight amid a welter of falling and surging bergs. Then we see the dot of its brilliant red hull and know it has survived. Bottom readings are clear. They show a depth of 350 meters (1,100 feet) close to the west side of the Johns Hopkins ice front. We have just charted an underwater canyon.

The Johns Hopkins Glacier started advancing more than 50 years ago. South of here the Brady

Ashore at Photo Station 3, marked by a cairn, Growler crew members try to ascertain changes in glacier positions.

Glacier extends a full 70 kilometers (43 miles) through the Fairweather Range to Taylor Bay. Indeed, the Reid Glacier and the Lamplugh, near the mouth of this inlet, are lobes of the Brady. It is an ice mass today choking a fjord, much as ice a few centuries ago sealed the Glacier Bay fjord, forcing out the *Tchukanedi* Tlingits and denying entrance to Captain Vancouver. Why the asynchrony? Why, of the national park's 17 current tidewater glaciers, are six advancing, three retreating, and eight holding their own?

Photo Station 3: We have rowed ashore on the west side of Johns Hopkins Inlet to photograph the glaciers from a position first used decades ago by Dr. William O. Field, of the American Geographical Society. This station is simply a rounded, glacier-polished outcrop of white rock partly veneered by a mat of dryas runners rooted nearby. A low stone cairn holds a jar with a registry of those who have made official photographs here. It requests anyone who takes unofficial pictures to send copies to the Society to enhance the record. There are only four entries, beginning with 1958. The position is stunning. We see the Johns Hopkins and Gilman Glaciers clearly and half a dozen high peaks, including Mount Crillon, almost 4,000 meters (13,000 feet) high.

I talked with Dr. Field a few years ago in New York City. White haired, the epitome of a gentleman-scholar, he is dean of those who have studied Alaskan glaciers. From memory he recited which glaciers were advancing, which retreating, and in what years. As a young geographer he had pondered the small amount of ice left in the United States compared to its dominant role in shaping the land. "That's when I got hooked," he told me.

In 1926 on his first trip to Glacier Bay he noticed immense changes in the ice positions documented by pioneering glaciologists beginning in the late 1800s. Harry Reid, for example, had written about "changes expected in the next 50 years." Where Reid's map showed solid ice, Field watched whales and seals. The ice was gone.

"You need continuity in a record," he told me. "Otherwise there's no way to see what's happening. The Johns Hopkins Glacier, for example, has advanced a mile since I first saw it in 1926 and it's still coming. Small glaciers show change more quickly

These pictures taken by William O. Field from Photo Station 3 document the advancing position of the Johns Hopkins Glacier in (top to bottom) August of 1941, 1950, and 1976. This glacier began its current advance about 50 years ago. Use the mountain peaks as reference points to verify the advance for yourself. Nearby Gilman Glacier, and a small hanging glacier on Mt. Abbe, above the Johns Hopkins, have hardly changed since the 1930s.

Professor Field sets up for theodolite readings from a survey station near Muir Glacier in 1976.

than vast icefields can. Greater accumulation than normal, or more melting, and they respond almost right away. Yet glaciers aren't simply barometers of climate. There's more to it, especially with tidewater glaciers."

The lack of glacier documentation had launched Field's career. Getting data takes remarkable persistence, partly because of the mammoth compilation needed and partly because of isolated and difficult working conditions.

"You need triangulation to keep track of what an ice front is doing, but maintaining usable triangulation points gets tough at times," Dr. Field reminisced. "You may go back and find a station worthless because alder has grown so much you can't see out, let alone do any surveying or even take a picture.

"Or if the ice is advancing, you have to move the station out of its way. If it's receding, you still have to move so as to stay close enough to do any good. In the 1940s we watched the Grand Pacific Glacier advance from Canada back into the U.S. We'd set up a station and it'd be obliterated before we could get back on another trip. Access was a problem, too, even if the station was still there. We had a real battle getting to the photo point between the Margerie and the Grand Pacific. The beach we needed to land on often was completely blocked by floating icebergs. And the calving of new ones set up shock waves that kept us alert the times we did go ashore."

Field said that tidewater glaciers "confuse the whole picture" in measuring past climates. As an oversimplification, assume the steady nourishing of a glacier by yearly snowfall. Once equilibrium is reached, this ice should neither thicken nor thin, advance nor retreat. Given present climate, this fairly well describes most ice tongues in Glacier Bay National Park and Preserve except for those that reach saltwater. These cause the confusion, but research aboard *Growler* has contributed to understanding them. Receding tidewater glaciers reach into deep water. Advancing or stable tongues end either on marine shoals or where the heads of inlets rise above sea level.

If deep water spells retreat, what's the depth where tidal glaciers are advancing? Shallow. Usually less than 80 meters (260 feet).

Why? The glaciers themselves make it so. They

Tidewater Glaciers

A tidewater glacier is one whose snout touches tidal water, such as Glacier Bay. Sixteen glaciers actively calve icebergs into tidal water in the park. This painting—based on the Johns Hopkins Glacier—shows you the dynamics and effects of such a mammoth ice sheet from near its high-mountain origins to the submarine sole of its snout. The submerged fjord walls and floor are interpreted from contour lines plotted from bathymetric readings taken aboard the research vessel *Growler* (see

photos on pages 24 and 29). An advancing glacier is like a combined bulldozer and conveyor belt. It cuts and shoves material around, and conveys it forward from the mountains; Johns Hopkins Glacier began its current advance some 50 years ago. To support its advance, a tidewater glacier builds a protective shoal at its snout by dumping rock debris. Plucking material from the up-slope of this ridge and depositing it on the down-slope enable the glacier to advance in deep water. This balance is precarious. The least retreat may back it off the shoal. Rapid retreat then sets in until it again reaches shallow water, usually the head of tidewater. These characteristics make tidewater glaciers poor measures of climate change.

advance only if they've built a protective shoal at the snout, by dumping rock debris. This forms an underwater terminal moraine and provides a partial barrier between the ice and the erosive action of sea water. By plucking material from the up-slope of this ridge and redepositing it on the down-slope, a glacier can keep advancing along even a very deep waterway.

How fast? Perhaps one to three kilometers (0.5 to 2 miles) per century. Eventually the ice may become so extended that the amount lost from the surface melt and calving matches the snowfall feeding the upper glacier. At this stage, balance is so precarious that even a slight retreat causes the snout to back off its shoal and re-enter deep water. Irreversible retreat then continues until the glacier reaches shallow water, usually at the head of tidewater. There it stabilizes, at least until it builds enough shoal to begin a new, slow advance.

Sometimes I resent the name Johns Hopkins for this inlet. It comes from an early-day university expedition here. It struck me as audacious to make an institutional trophy of such scenic magnificence. Bob Howe, park superintendent when I first visited here, clamped a moratorium on further naming of peaks, valleys, waterfalls—or anything. He felt there should be places where humans experience the pristine without presuming to label. The gift shop manager of a cruise ship told me she put up a *closed* sign during her first trip into Johns Hopkins Inlet. "Come to the upper deck if you need film," her note read. "The shop will reopen after we leave Johns Hopkins." It's that beautiful.

Reid Inlet: We anchored *Growler* about 0200 this morning. We'd eaten another midnight dinner after finishing the Johns Hopkins depth readings and hiking across the Topeka Glacier outwash, looking for fossil wood. We debated whether to stay in Johns Hopkins or run to Reid Inlet. Austin decided to run because we might be too tired to stand effective watch through the night. There was too little pack ice in Johns Hopkins Inlet to hold *Growler* safely free of the sidewalls as we drifted. Two other vessels also were running, their distant lights ghostly companions for the late, weary hour. One must have been *Explorer*, the park concession boat that drifts in the pack ice off the Margerie Glacier through half the night, giving passengers a unique experience of

the upper bay. The other probably was a commercial fishing boat.

Harry Reid's 1890 map of this inlet now bearing his name shows nothing but ice here. No land at all. Even in the 1940s, when Joe and Muz Ibach built a distinctive little cabin and began mining pockets of gold ore high on the cliffs, the Reid Glacier had drawn back no farther than the toe of their beach. Now you can boat 6 kilometers (4 miles) into the inlet.

After breakfast this morning we motored *Growler's* dory across from our anchorage, following as close as is prudent to the bulging ice face. "The glacier must be advancing," Austin said. "Look at the push moraines." He pointed out low ridges of rock and gravel slightly ahead of where ice is pressing against the inlet's sidewall. Circular mats of dryas are half swallowed by the advance. Sheer crevasses split the ice where its leading edge has thrust across the land. They form 50-meter (164-foot) slits clearly visible against the sky.

Aboard *Growler* I have been seeing advancing or stable glaciers, yet other glaciers in the park are rapidly withdrawing. Muir Glacier has gone back 40 kilometers (25 miles) since 1890 when Reid mapped its terminus barely above the inlet's junction with Glacier Bay. In the years my husband, Louis, and I have been coming to the park we have seen the Muir front separate from the Riggs Glacier and retreat far up the inlet. Austin says it has only a few kilometers to go to reach the head of tidewater.

Elevation explains why some glaciers advance here while others withdraw. Tarr, Johns Hopkins, and Reid Inlets all finger from exceedingly high peaks. Plateaus feeding their ice typically stand 2,000 meters (6,500 feet) high and are subject to prodigious snowfall. The park's retreating glaciers, on the other hand, derive from elevations averaging about half that high. The uplands near Glacier Bay's mouth, where ice is gone, rise little more than 350 meters (1,100 feet) overall. This difference in park elevations separates northwestern advancing ice from eastern receding ice. And the Brady Icefield's immensity seems to influence its own weather. The icefield chills moisture-laden clouds from the Pacific and triggers their glacier-nourishing release.

Surprisingly small temperature differences account

for radically varying glacial effects. The Wisconsinan Ice Age was only 5 to 6 degrees Celsius cooler than today. The following warm period averaged perhaps one degree warmer than today. During the Little Ice Age here, the elevation above which more snow fell in winter than melted in summer was about 830 meters (2,700 feet). Dr. Field places this point today at 1,600 meters (5,200 feet)—except for the Brady Icefield where it's half that.

No wonder the only glaciers here likely to advance now are those with their heads high in the mountains. The dice are hopelessly loaded against the others, aside from the peculiarities of tidewater ice. Viewed on a time scale of millennia, all glaciers are responding to climate. They are asynchronous only in terms of centuries and decades, time scales more comprehensible because they better match our lifespan. What we view as significant events may be minute fluctuations on the millennial scale, which is, for glaciers, the more true scale.

Post-Glacier Plant Succession

Harebells (front) and fire-weed push up their colors from streamside rock rubble tumbled like fist-sized gems by past torrents of glacial meltwater.

In Muir Inlet: A photograph taken in the 1890s shows an excursion steamer at the Muir ice front and, perched closeby on a completely barren moraine, the one-room cabin where John Muir hosted Harry Reid's research party. Today the cabin is just an overgrown heap of chimney stones and from the place where the photo was taken you can't even see out through the alder and spruce. As for the glacier snout, it's now 40 kilometers (25 miles) away. Just as glaciologists find these inlets ideal for pinpointing the coming and going of ice, botanists revel in the chance to document the plants' green conquest of denuded landscapes retreating glaciers leave behind.

My husband, Louis, and I were at the Muir snout this afternoon with Chess Lyons, aboard our small sloop, *Taku*. At 7 meters (23 feet) long, *Taku* is outclassed by some icebergs we sailed among. We brought the sloop to Juneau by ferry and then sailed and motored to Glacier Bay. Louis is a skilled sailor so enamored of the sea that I suspect saltwater, not blood, flows in his veins. Our friend Chess has no sailing background but his career as naturalist with British Columbia Provincial Parks—he is now retired—and maker of nature films has given him abundant outdoor experience. I am adept in the galley, less so in the cockpit, yet enthusiastic about life afloat, whether aboard *Growler* last month or now *Taku*. We ate today's lunch while sailing up the inlet, wind flicking salad from our bowls. Even without sails raised, *Taku* heeled ten degrees. With sails, we traveled faster than *Taku's* rated hull speed of seven knots.

Yesterday we motored to the head of Wachusett Inlet, a Muir tributary. The lower part of Wachusett Inlet, longest free of glacier ice, is green with vegetation while utter barrenness still characterizes the newly ice-free upper reaches. At the head of the inlet we hiked to the divide separating Wachusett from Queen Inlet. This took us backward through vegetation's green chronology: The lower the slope, the more recent the plants. Hiking at first was like crossing a desert alluvial fan except that we found *no* plants. Even in Death Valley you can't take a dozen steps without coming on greenery. Here was nothing but sand and rock. The land is virgin, newly released from the ice.

A bit higher I finally noticed a plant, a single fireweed half a finger high. Soon other fireweed plants and equally tiny willows were present. Upslope the plants gradually got taller and the willow even had branches. We added scouring rush to the species list we were keeping, then dryas. The dryas stood a centimeter (0.4 inches) high, each plant having six leaves. I kept the lens cap on my camera because the plants were so widespread and puny that footsteps kicked up dust.

The vegetation changed abruptly as we reached a high terrace that had been free of ice substantially longer than the slopes below. The willow now reached halfway to our knees. Leathery-leafed dryas plants formed circular mats, and cushions of dark, dry moss padded spaces between alders growing as high as my shoulder. At the divide we found Christmas-tree spruce and carpets of heather. We had walked backward through plant succession, beaching our dinghy on land born just two years ago and climbing to a surface now green, but new a century ago when Harry Reid made his glacier map and John Muir explored the inlet that bears his name.

Plant beginnings may be no more than "black crust," a cohesive feltlike nap believed to be mostly algae. This helps stabilize silt and hold in moisture. Moss adds thicker, more conspicuous tufts to the covering, and windblown spores and seeds of plants from scouring rush to fireweed and willow, spruce, and alder arrive and root. Along beaches, seeds such as those of ryegrass ride ashore on extreme high tides. Blueberry and crowberry seeds get deposited in bird feces, the seedlings thereby benefitting from minute dots of fertilizer. Bears and wolves and mountain goats, shaking water from their pelts, may shake out clinging seeds picked up where they last fed. Campers sweeping out tents may also contribute. By such means, vegetation's green conquest makes its start.

Successful growth depends in part on where the

In raw landscapes dryas builds soil and adds enriching nitrogen. Fossil and pollen studies show that this matting plant pioneered much of Europe and North America when the last Ice Age ended.

seeds happen to land. Glacier till and outwash are notoriously deficient in nitrogen and at first produce stunted, yellowish plant growth. Green exceptions to this rule are alder and dryas. Both solve the problem by associating with micro-organisms that draw nitrogen directly from the air. Alder relies on molds living on its roots in nodules about the size of grain kernels or sometimes as big as walnuts. Dryas roots apparently interrelate with mycorrhizae, minute fungi that sheathe the roots of many plant species and stimulate growth in ways not fully understood. The process seems to involve enzyme and nitrogen production.

Fossil leaves, seed hairs, and pollen recovered in bogs and excavations indicate that dryas pioneered much of northern Europe and America at the close of the last Ice Age. Their first year the plants produce single rosettes of tiny leaves. The next year this growth triples; the third year it quadruples. Mats well over a meter (a yard) across develop after five years. At this stage, lateral shoots rapidly fuse individual mats into massive carpets.

Sitka alder *(Alnus crispa)* begins to dominate suitable sites within a couple of decades following glacier retreat. It eventually forms dense stands that are abominably tangled—and disliked by humans who are afoot. At this stage trees are about 3 meters (10 feet) high, the limbs of individual alders growing low and wickedly interlocked. Hike through such thickets and you find arms, legs, shoulders, eyeglasses, bracelet, and backpack each caught separately and pulled in differing directions. You can't see out. Holding to a course is largely luck without a compass. Brown/grizzly bear tracks thread what openings there are, then vanish. The more you try to see where the tracks lead, the more certain it is that your noisy bashing about will startle a ptarmigan, the explosive whirr of its wings all but stopping your heart until its gravelly *tobacco-tobacco-tobacco* call registers an all-clear: bird, not bear.

"Two of us after three hours of thrashing through this dreaded shrub, emerged at the point where we had set out!" lamented a recent British researcher. But alder has its good side. It stimulates the growth of other plants. Its fallen leaves put as much nitrogen into the soil as alfalfa would. Dryas similarly enriches the soil. Alder and dryas are such successful plant pioneers and become so dominant that you'd expect

Post-Glacial Plant Succession

After glacial retreat, vegetation recolonizes bare, nutrient-poor land in successive stages. Algal plant associations stabilize silt. Moss tufts follow. Then come scouring rush and fireweed, or dryas, a matting plant that pioneered post-Ice Age Europe and North America. Willow, alder, and spruce next gain footholds. The climax stage is the mature spruce-hemlock forest found at Bartlett Cove.

Ryegrass (large photo) may pioneer beaches. Inset photos (clockwise from upper left) show: alder, cottonwood, hemlock, and spruce.

Plants Recover the Landscape

For two centuries glacial ice has been melting back in retreat up this fjord we know as Glacier Bay. This means that none of the plant life seen here today is more than 200 years old. Most of it is indeed far younger.

At Bartlett Cove, the full 200 years have allowed development of mature spruce forest. Within this forest more than one generation of trees has had time to grow, many old veterans have died, and fungi and molds have become established in the special habitat of decaying wood. Further up the fjord the number of plants decreases. Living conditions loom more severe and habitats are fewer. At the fjord's farthest reaches, at the ice margins themselves, are only mosses, lichens, and primitive plants struggling to reclaim raw land for coming stages of revegetation.

It is difficult to imagine that the landscape of richly forested Barlett Cove was so recently similar to the glacier rubble of the stream-cut terminal moraine shown at right. However, the setting of this stream, issuing from a nearby retreating glacier, repeats the scene that has been marching up-bay for two centuries.

Red columbine

Moss

Blueberry

Terminal moraine succession

Baneberry, two types

Fungus

Bitter cress

Skunk cabbage

them to last forever. Their growth is so dense, however, that their own progeny can't make headway. Their role is to stabilize and enrich the soil. That done, they die out and a comparative explosion of plant diversity ensues.

Overall, this successional drama is similar along the shorelands of all up-bay country. First come the scattered pioneers, succeeded by a low-growing mat stage and then a thicket stage. The two major arms of the Glacier Bay waterway differ, however, in their rates of development within these stages and in the species playing key roles. In Muir Inlet and its tributaries alder is ubiquitous. In the upper Tarr Inlet drainage alder thrives only in swales and draws. Soapberry and willow approximate a thicket stage, one you can easily hike through.

These geographic differences are surprisingly clear cut. In Muir Inlet a land surface that has been free of ice nearly a century will host a formidable tangle of alder—or be well along toward spruce forest. But in Tarr Inlet, dryas and willow still will dominate a surface of comparable age. Why should Muir Inlet be ahead in its plant sequences? Probably because it opens toward the prevailing southerly wind. This may simplify the arrival of seeds and spores, and moderate temperatures. Harsh Tarr Inlet conditions contrast markedly. Ocean-born moist winds are blocked by the Fairweather mountains, which send cold, dry air draining downslope from the high peaks.

From *Growler*, we regularly rowed ashore so that Emily Chase could core trees for a study, counting annual rings to find out how long it takes for a surface freed of ice to become upholstered by full forest. In the park, Bartlett Cove, which is edged by a Little Ice Age terminal moraine, has been evolving toward forest the longest. It melted out a bit before Captain Vancouver arrived offshore. Its forest now is a stately mix of Sitka spruce and western hemlock. The forest floor is thickly padded by moss and clubmoss and is studded with fern, blueberry, devil's club, and twayblade.

On Young Island, only a few kilometers up the bay from Bartlett Cove and therefore free of ice only about two centuries, we sank ankle deep into chartreuse moss which extended from the forest floor onto the stubby lower branches of spruce. The trunks of these trees were bigger than one person alone could encircle with outstretched arms. The only hemlock we happened to find had a diameter less than half that of most of the spruce. On Francis Island, spruce were mere dark pyramids barely beginning to overtop thick cottonwoods, and we saw no hemlock. There, we pulled ourselves up steep slopes by alder and willow branches. We had moved 30 kilometers (19 miles) up-bay from Bartlett Cove, sampling forests separated by about twelve decades of growth opportunity.

Spruce arrive and sprout early in Glacier Bay's plant sequence, but they grow slowly at first. A 30- to 40-year-old tree may stand only knee high yet have a trunk as thick as a man's ankle. Its time is coming. Eventually it dominates for a century or two, then is outnumbered by hemlock, providing events follow a classic course for plant succession here. On the outer coast, however, not all spruce forests even wait for the ice to melt. The forest actually grows like a green rug atop the stagnant Fairweather Glacier tongue and on remnants of the Lituya Glacier, flourishing because lowland glaciers characteristically carry heavy mineral loads. Spruce and even good-sized hemlock stand rooted in thick soil and duff. But they tilt drunkenly because pits form in the underlying ice and meltwater grottoes collapse.

Muskeg is the final stage of plants' green conquest in southeast Alaska, though none exists along Glacier Bay National Park and Preserve's inner waterways. Sufficient time has not elapsed since withdrawal of the Little Ice Age glaciers. Muskeg represents a wondrous coming full circle, a return to openness though not to barrenness. It develops as forest soil deteriorates after 500 to 1,000 years, building a hardpan layer that blocks drainage and prevents roots from anchoring securely. Mature trees consequently topple readily during wind storms, creating openings which encourage other plants. Saturated conditions preclude most bacteria and fungi, retarding decay. Instead, sufficient organic litter accumulates to hold year-round moisture even without the hardpan layer, which slowly disintegrates. Acid conditions prevail and vegetation changes from forest to muskeg.

Along the park's outer coast are lowlands that escaped being covered by ice during the last glacier

Plant succession will culminate in spruce-hemlock forest in most of the park. The forest floor near park headquarters at Bartlett Cove still shelters glacial clues, however. Hollows betray where abandoned ice blocks took years and years to melt. Moss-covered hummocks disguise sandy glacial outwash.

advance. They have been muskeg for at least 8,000 years, changing very little through most of this time. New species continually arrive and vie for optimum position during the two or three centuries that lead up to the spruce-hemlock stage. But once muskeg takes over, little changes. Spruce and western hemlock continue, but grow scattered and dwarfed and with a look of great age and adversity. Mountain hemlock, lodgepole pine, and in places yellow cedar, come in. Beneath them a variety of soggy and leathery-leaved species forms a rough upholstery. The mood of muskeg is elfin, mysterious.

Just east of Glacier Bay, muskeg grows at Point Couverden, the Home Shore that gave refuge to Tlingits fleeing the Little Ice Age glacier encroaching upon their Valley of the River Grass. En route from Juneau Louis, Chess, and I anchored *Taku* overnight in the point's lee and I rowed ashore. Walking inland I passed first through beachside ryegrass and head-high cow parsnip flower stalks left from last season. Then I passed through a band of spruce-hemlock forest rich with fern. Ahead I could see the rounded tops of lodgepole pine, a clear contrast to the sharp spires of spruce and the pointed-but-drooping tops of hemlock. Abruptly, the forest gave way to open, mossy, soggy muskeg. Pines grew scattered and interspersed with a few stunted mountain hemlock. Deer fern replaced the lady fern and wood fern I'd noticed in the forest, and hip-high bushes of bog laurel and Labrador tea mixed with enormous blueberry bushes laden with fruit the size of giant peas. I could pick five or six powdery-blue berries at a time without moving my hand. For the first time I can remember it didn't matter if a berry dropped. We had blueberry pancakes for breakfast.

Tidal Inlet: The wind has died. Louis and Chess and I are motoring up Tidal Inlet in *Taku*, savoring the last of the daylight. Waterfall Fjord would be an appropriate name here. Every few minutes we come to another falls. Most spill over the cliffs, unnamed and rarely seen. Ribbons of white, cascades, plumes. One as lacy as Yosemite's Bridal Veil Falls, deep-set in a rock vee. Another showy only at the bottom, where it splashes from six separate ledges. A third hits so hard it spurts up and out. From the side you see only an odd, gravity-defying spout of white water.

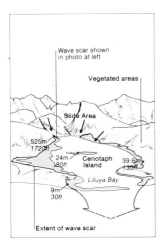

Wave scar shown in photo at left

Vegetated areas

Slide Area

525m
1720ft

24m
80ft

Cenotaph
Island

39.6m
130ft

Lituya Bay

9m
30ft

Extent of wave scar

A 1958 earthquake triggered a landslide at Lituya Bay's upper end. The slide created a wave that denuded the promontory facing it (shown at the left in the photo of Lituya Glacier) to an altitude of 525 meters (1,720 feet). Three boats were in the bay. The island protected one. A second washed over the sandspit at the bay's mouth and into the ocean. The third was destroyed. The drawing shows the extent of denuded shorelines.

High above us, the fjord wall is gashed by a raw arc, the scar of a gigantic landslide, that stretches for more than 2 kilometers (1 mile) and looks as high as a six- or eight-story building. It is ten times that.

Austin Post once told me the scar formed as ice choking the inlet retreated, withdrawing support and leaving an over-steepened slope. This probably happened around 1860-70. Parts of the scar have stabilized enough for alders to grow, but the whole slope looks poised to slide more—and it probably does slide a little whenever there's an earthquake.

We cruise along sipping brandy aboard *Taku* and contemplating earth forces capable of suddenly resetting the clock of life's sequences. Were this slide to let go and crash into saltwater, a stupendous wave would strip vegetation far beyond reach of the slide itself. That happened at Lituya Bay in July 1958. A quake along the Fairweather Fault, at the upper end of the bay, dislodged rain-soaked rubble from a steep headwall. This material sheared off ice at the snout of the Lituya Glacier, then, riding an air cushion, shot across the toe of an adjacent cliff to an elevation of 525 meters (1,700 feet). The force hurled icebergs and seals onto high ledges and violently uprooted mature spruce. Displaced water rose as an incredible wave that ravaged shores even at the mouth of the bay, 11 kilometers (7 miles) from the headwall. The wave lifted a fishing boat, swept it across the moraine guarding Lituya Bay's entrance, and smacked it down in the ocean so forcefully the seams burst and the boat disassembled, fortunately not before the couple aboard could leap into their skiff and row off.

From the air the devastated Lituya Bay cliff scar is astonishing. Uprooted trees litter every beach of the bay. Seen from a boat, the destruction appears even more dramatic. Its full magnitude is immediate, without the detachment a plane affords. The soil, forest, glacial till, rock, and ice that slid into the water is estimated at nearly 400 million cubic meters (1.3 billion cubic feet). This appalling mass sent a wave racing down-bay probably 250 kilometers (155 miles) per hour and exerting sufficient pressure to splinter trees and rip mussels and barnacles from their holds. Lituya Bay shorelands for a kilometer (half mile) inland still have recovered only to the alder stage.

Four earlier giant waves—1936, 1899, 1874, 1854 —can still be traced by tree damage. Heights ranged from some 20 meters (65 feet) to about 130 meters (425 feet)—gentle foretastes of July 1958. Doubtless there have been others, and giant waves remain certain for the bay's future, perhaps soon. Slopes where the 1958 slide broke loose are still unstable and a separate huge inverted vee of unconsolidated earth hangs on a cliff near the North Crillon Glacier. This new headwall slippage already seems to defy gravity.

Bedrock geology is responsible for such slippages. The 1958 quake registered eight on the Richter scale and produced a 7-meter (23-foot) horizontal displacement along the Fairweather Fault. With the edge of the oceanic plate slipping beneath the continental plate and wrinkling the edge into mountain ranges, earthquakes are inevitable. Given the walled-in nature of fjords, so are the consequent devastating waves. The shifting along the junction of the oceanic and continental plates is a tectonic ("building") process. The Earth's crust is built of adjoining plates which float on a molten core. Uplift of the coast comes in jerks. Barnacles still cling where bellflowers and Indian paintbrushes bloom. The change from tidepool to cliff garden can be abrupt.

The coming and going of glaciers can also directly raise and lower both the ocean volume and the land surface. Worldwide sea level during the Wisconsinan Ice Age stood about 100 meters (325 feet) lower than it does today. It rose as the glaciers melted and released water to the oceans. If Earth's ice were all to melt, sea level would rise far more. Fish would swim Tokyo's Ginza. Sea anemones would wave from Manhattan's World Trade Center.

Evidence of sea-level fluctuation along the park's outer coast includes a wave-cut terrace 30 meters (100 feet) above present tide line. Because the terrace is recognizable on both sides of the Fairweather Fault, tectonic force cannot explain its origin. Most likely it formed during sea-level changes produced by glacier ice. Ice a kilometer or two (0.5 or 1.3 miles) thick is enough to depress bedrock. Melting releases this weight, and the land slowly rebounds, or rises.

In Glacier Bay, the rate of rebound is greater than

anywhere else in southeast Alaska, and even by worldwide standards it is spectacular. At Bartlett Cove rebound now produces a 4-centimeter (1.5-inch) rise per year. On the nature trail near the lodge, where you drop down the stairs from mature spruce-hemlock forest into a zone of young spruce and beach meadow, you step onto land newly raised from the sea. The base of the stairs marks the old high tide line. Count a sapling's growth rings, then add time for salt to wash from the beach and for spruce to germinate, and you can know about how long ago the surface changed from sea bottom to dry land. Up-bay, release from the weight of the ice is more recent than at Bartlett Cove and present rebound is even more rapid. The shorelands rising fastest now are those close to the mouth of Muir Inlet, where glacier retreat began only about a century ago.

With rebound, islands expand noticeably, decade by decade, and shoal water shifts, quickly rendering inshore marine charts useless. Tide zones and beach meadows are constantly born anew. And humans experience certain dilemmas. For example, the land has risen so decidedly that National Park Service employees now can get their boats to and from the headquarters dock only when full high tide floods the channel. At Gustavus, the politics grow tangled, for who owns virgin land? Once the gravel of these flatlands formed the fill in Muir Inlet. Swept southward, that gravel lay beneath the sea for millennia. Now the land has risen and we humans puzzle over its ownership.

"So Far As Known"

This personable harbor seal pup has hauled out on an iceberg. Why not? It was probably born on one; scientists think this is a recent adaptation here.

Field notebooks of summers in the 1970s document hour-by-hour seal behavior in Johns Hopkins and Muir Inlets. Summer park biologist John McConnell:

"*16 June, 2:14 p.m.* Earthquake tremor! Two-second duration. Ground shook. Rocks fell off north side of Inlet. Seals calling all over now. Not much diving in. Just up, looking around. Pretty loud boom that echoes. No calving on either Muir or Riggs.

"*2:34 p.m.* Lost pup has been swimming around calling for about 10 minutes. Hauls out. Back in, and goes on swimming and calling frantically. No one seems to care.... One really LOUD call, almost scream.

"*2:42 p.m.* Pup really frantic. One single adult in water about 60 yards away looking around and raising out of water to look. Could this be the negligent mother?

"*2:45 p.m.* Lost pup comes up to mother-pup pair on berg, calling. Looks. They don't even wake up.

"*2:48 p.m.* Single adult swimming in direction of lost pup.

"*2:50 p.m.* Come together, bump noses, pup shuts up and they dive, come up, now swimming off to north. Crisis ended.

"*17 June, 4:20 p.m.* Mother and two pups playing; they all ball up and roll over and over, then dive, come up, and do it again. Both pups alternate hitching rides on her back till she rolls them off. Mother goes to each and bumps noses.

"*4:24 p.m.* Here comes a single adult toward the threesome. Goes to one pup, touches noses. Now swims off with that pup. Other female and pup go in different direction. Was it a Muir Inlet baby sitting service I watched a moment ago?"

Former park biologist Greg Streveler one summer counted 3,500 seals in Johns Hopkins Inlet. Nearly a third that many ride the floating ice of upper Muir Inlet. When glaciers were still discharging bergs into

Wachusett and Adams Inlets, seal pupping took place there as well, but the pupping went out with the ice. Hair seals congregate in their pupping grounds from May to August where the pack ice is thickest. Seals probably adapted to pupping on floating ice only since the last glacier retreat; before that pupping on beaches and rocky islets. Greg explains why biologists think this:

"Seals hauled out onto ice seem to worry more about what's going on along the shore than what's happening in the water nearby. A man on the beach, even 150 meters (500 feet) away, will panic mothers and pups into diving off their bergs. But once they're in the water their terror eases. The animals seem genetically coded to be more wary of trouble coming from the land than from the water. They must have moved to floating ice as an escape from shore predators, but they haven't yet perfected new behavior to go with the habitat."

Greg also says that the mother's pattern of searching for her separated pup would work far better along the fixed shore than it does in the shifting realm of floating ice. Indeed, this is the weak point in mother-pup bonds. Lost pups soon become dead pups. People should never approach seals closer than 50 meters (160 feet) during the critical early weeks of pupping in mid-May to late June. Killer whales, supposedly hair seals' greatest enemy, don't go to the heads of Johns Hopkins or Muir Inlets. It is ironic that people, armed only with cameras and often good intentions, should pose such a threat.

"It's being startled that has the grave implications," Greg says. "That's what leads to separation."

Geike Inlet: We've anchored at Shag Cove, just inside Geike Inlet, where Chess immediately rigged his pole and cast from *Taku's* cockpit. He said he'd add this spot to his world map of places he's caught no fish. I've just rowed back from watching salmon by the thousands struggle up the creek to spawn in freshwater. They rarely feed while spawning.

Salmon spawning is a spectacle: Carcasses line the creek banks, heads a sepulchral white, hooked jaws still full of needle teeth, eye sockets empty. Live fish thrash against the water's flow, backs above the surface, wriggling like snakes, forcing passage over cobbles. Sometimes they turn on their sides and slither up shallow riffles. Pale underbellies show.

Yellow eyes seem strained and desperate.

Once a sudden movement and a loud splash made me pivot to look. A huge male had wedged head-down between two rocks, caught by water pouring forcefully over a log. I watched his struggle, then looked away. When I turned back, he'd broken free. I counted 33 fish in a 3-meter (10-foot) radius. This entire cove was deep beneath ice 150 years ago. When the glacier began to wane, runoff streams must have carried more silt than fish tolerate. When did the salmon arrive?

Once Louis and I joined Ole Wik in checking on whether Dolly Varden had returned to a stream at the head of Geike Inlet, not far from Shag Cove. My journal of that trip with Ole records:

"We sit in the dinghy halfway to shore, attention riveted on a half-grown wolf pup that trots from where it was feeding. It watches us from the willows, secure within their protective screen although keeping ears cocked like twin radars.

"After a while, the pup moves on, then returns with a second pup. Both are black, typical of wolves in Glacier Bay—and not an unexpected color, for wolves as a whole vary from sand-colored, through almost red, to this decided black. The two pups stand curious, but unconcerned. For once, there is time to focus binoculars and fix a sight indelibly in mind

"While the wolves stare at us, a whale rolls barely astern of our anchored boat. It blows, smacks the water with a flipper so long it's like a wing; then the whale submerges. The sudden slap against the water startles 200 to 300 crows into circling as a ragged black cloud, cawing wildly. Their racket prompts a bald eagle into lifting off from somewhere so far back in the spruce that we wouldn't have noticed it if it hadn't flown.

"Where but Glacier Bay can you swivel binoculars and find such a three-minute sequence of land, sea, and air life as prelude for a stream check? We find no Dolly Varden, however. Maybe conditions aren't yet right. Maybe our seasonal timing is off."

Glacier streams raging across raw outwash plains attract no salmon. But in time as stream conditions mature, fish find their way. With them a whole chain of life is fostered. Eagles, ravens, and coyotes feed on spawned-out salmon carcasses littering the banks.

The Salmon Economy

Salmon annually succumb to a bizarre frenzy approximating the behavior they routinely incite in anglers. Natural predators catch this short-lived fever, too. For the brief season of the salmon spawning run, birds and mammals line the banks and plunge into streams to gorge on live fish or spawned-out carcasses. A stable and diverse ecology seems to convert overnight to a one-crop marketplace, the protein-rich salmon economy. Silver, chum, sockeye, and pink salmon spawn in the park streams. Poised to pounce and peck, or to pluck them from streams and banks, are bald eagles (inset), ravens, coyotes, wolves, minks, otters, seals, black bears, and brown/grizzly bears. Some predators and their prey even seem to observe a tacit truce

Silver (coho) salmon

Chum salmon, female

Sockeye salmon, female

during the run. In close quarters they grab what they can from this small end of an ephemeral gourmet funnel. Pragmatically seen, nature would appear to transfer food wealth from the oceans into a protein-starved terrestrial food chain. The uncanny homing ability of salmon—after years at sea they find the same stream gravels in which they were born—remains one of nature's great intrigues.

Pink (humpback) salmon

Chum salmon, male

Sockeye salmon, male

Mink and otter, wolves, black bears and brown/grizzly bears take live fish. Seals foray into stream mouths to feed on spawners newly arrived at homewater.

Four Pacific salmon species spawn here: silver, chum, sockeye, and pink. Dolly Varden, steelhead, cutthroat, and three-spined stickleback also spawn in Glacier Bay's freshwater. King salmon frequent Bartlett Cove, Berg Bay, and Dundas Bay, but do not yet enter streams to spawn, s.f.a.k. — "so far as known," as field naturalists a century ago acknowledged the limits of their knowledge.

Details can prove fascinating. In some Glacier Bay streams snails and bivalves are few because the water is too low in dissolved minerals for the making of shells. Shells are mostly calcium carbonate. On the other hand, tiny shrimplike creatures thrive in ephemeral ponds fed by melt from glacier remnants. Their eggs don't dry out readily and will pass unscathed through the guts of fish or birds. In fact, viable eggs have been found in the feces of fish-eating birds. This means the eggs have endured a double dose of gut acids, first the fish's, then the bird's!

Birds bring crustaceans to newly formed ponds. Insects come on their own, to streams as well as ponds. The aquatic nymphs of mayflies, stoneflies, and caddisflies are equipped with bristles, hooks, and suckers for clinging to rocks, so rushing water is no problem. Various biting flies are equally able to survive immature stream conditions. Even close to melting ice in water too cold, rushing, and silt laden for other species, blackfly larvae secure themselves to rocks by hooking their tails into specially secreted silken pads. "No-see-ums," perpetrators of painful bites in their adult stage, also flourish in glacial torrents. Ashore in summer, you scarcely escape their swarming attack anywhere. Afloat you are safe.

"A sinuous strip a quarter of a mile wide on the landward side of the beach and double that to the sea is where the action is," Greg Streveler says. We owe the variety and abundance of wildlife in the park to this shoreland strip. The shore is the land mammal's larder because it links the sea's riches to life on land. Red foxes feed along the beach on ducks, sand fleas, gooseneck barnacles, dead fish, beached whales, fledglings, strawberries. Coyotes crunch open sea urchins and mussels. Greg once watched a brown/grizzly bear dig clams on the outer coast, "sand and rocks really flying, its butt sticking up out of the hole." Black bears squish open barnacles to eat. Shrews feast on barnacles, mussels, and squashed snails. Mountain goats and porcupines eat seaweed. Deer do too, but they can't digest it; deer have starved to death here, their stomachs full of seaweed. Sedges and grasses, available even in winter, bring the deer and goats to the shore. Seaweed is just a salty sidedish.

Shorebirds join the beach community while retreating glacier fronts are still closeby and floating bergs a constant presence. Oystercatchers—the size of northern crows, black with naked pink legs like stilts, and with bright orange, chopstick bills—are my favorites. They eat not oysters, but snails and mussels. Louis and I camped at Reid Inlet once and filmed oystercatcher hide-and-seek among small, stranded icebergs.

It was a gray June week with the mists clamped to the water. Sky and sea, equally wet, differed only in texture: the water polished, the clouds dull. For brief periods when the murk thinned we could make out a vee of scoters flying low to the water in one direction. Glaucous-winged gulls, higher, moved in the opposite direction. Or a fleet of pigeon guillemots might be bobbing as if at anchor, each bird a solid black fore and aft but with white wing patches separating end from end. When the guillemots dove after fish, their red legs and feet flashed a momentary finale to the upending.

Mew gulls and arctic terns nested on the foreshore, their eggs laid in saucer-shaped scrapings ungraced by grass, down, or other softening material. Gulls returning to brood duty often first landed on an iceberg to look around, their touchdowns like the uncontrolled skids of neophyte ice skaters. Arctic terns defended nests by dive-bombing and cursing intruders. Their targets included Louis and me, mew gulls, and the oystercatchers, which cringe comically when a tern zeroes in.

Louis and I knew that a pair of oystercatchers nested near the gulls and terns, but where? Both male and female stalked about glancing back to be sure we were fooled about where their nest was. Satisfied we were still watching, they then crouched and squirmed as though settling onto eggs.

One morning I chanced upon the two oystercatchers apparently at their real nest, well back from the highest strand line. They saw me see them. Looking chagrined and uncertain of what to do, they just shrieked and flew off. I retreated, stepping only on large flat stones to avoid crushing eggs I couldn't see. Their spotted shells blend perfectly with the rock mosaic left by a retreating glacier.

Arctic terns commute from Antarctic wintering grounds to Glacier Bay, arriving in May while snow still covers the ground. They are gone again by mid-August. To disrupt such hurried nesting and fledging would be unconscionable. The National Park Service grew concerned when the present large cruise ships began entering the bay. Excursion steamers of the late 1800s were much smaller. When the 33,000-ton *Arcadia* first arrived in 1970, rangers watched beaches to see what the ship's wake might do. A single errant wave could destroy nests and nullify the terns' 32,000-kilometer (20,000-mile) round-trip journey.

Fortunately, a ship moving slowly did no harm—probably less than our human presence ashore, no matter how carefully we stepped and stayed back photographing with long lenses. People are decidedly disturbing to wildlife. Wolves seem reluctant to trot their accustomed paths while people are around, though their scat shows they're still about. Mountain goats will abandon the whole side of a ridge facing a camp far below them.

That same summer of oystercatcher hide-and-seek Louis and I filmed at the Ohio State University research camp in Wachusett Inlet. Camp was a moonscape with ice. Tents sprouted from a bare moraine, icebergs floated past, and a kilometer (half mile) behind camp the stagnant Burroughs Glacier melted into oblivion. It shrank scores of meters (hundreds of feet) per year, its ice so brown with rock and silt that it hardly looked like a glacier. But terrestrial life had already begun staking a claim.

Snow buntings, trim white-bellied finches, came mornings to feed on iceworms, which look like wriggling bits of black thread. These distant relatives of earthworms live their whole lives in ice. There they feed on algae and bacteria, and on organic matter and minerals washed along by glacier-melt and borne by air currents. The first such worms

Birds of Sea and Shore

More than 200 species of birds have been recorded in the park. Many are best seen in or near marine environments, which offer them abundant and varied food. At bay mouths and in narrow waters, turbulence stirs up plankton, shrimp, and fish to the surface. For birds a feeding frenzy ensues. Critical protein sources come within diving and skimming distance of the water's surface. Large flocks of murrelets, kittiwakes, gulls, and northern phalaropes gather. Phalaropes are feminist: males wear the dull plumage and incubate the eggs. Phalaropes commute yearly far down into South America. Arctic terns commute up to 32,000 kilometers (20,000 miles) round trip each year.

Tufted and horned puffins

Horned grebe

Old squaw duck

Glaucous-winged gulls

Pigeon guillemot

Least sandpiper

Arctic terns

Kittiwake colony

79

Willow ptarmigan know camouflage. Both winter and summer, these birds blend so well with their surroundings that you may miss spotting them at arm's length. How many do you see in each picture?

reported anywhere—in 1877—came from the Muir Glacier. We now know iceworms occur widely in the coast mountains from Washington northward. A few years ago, Ohio State researchers flew iceworms home with them from Glacier Bay and maintained them in the laboratory for more than a year. In the esophagi of several, they found cylindrical micro-organisms which may secrete an enzyme that helps them digest algae. You never know where you'll find the base of a food chain.

One of the glaciologists found a dead shrew beneath the Burroughs Glacier when he roped down a cavernous melthole to trace water channels. Far out on the glacier taking measurements, two men were buzzed by a rufous hummingbird and several times saw bumblebees. Deer mice plagued the Wachusett camp at night. A tundra vole sampled every candy bar in one particular sack.

How can tiny rodents, hummingbirds, or bees brave the glacier barrens? Resilience and adaptations. Hummingbird metabolism permits a sustained energy output impossible among mammals. Bumblebees, far from hapless victims of environment, can control body temperature. Hike across a glacial outwash such as the one that spills from the Casement Glacier and at the ice face you find buntings pouring out territorial song from the sharp crests of eskers. Ptarmigan droppings are evident too. The birds blend so perfectly with rocks and moss tufts that you rarely see them unless and until they move.

Redpolls and rosy finches may be raiding willow catkins for seed and picking insects from where scattered fireweed and alder pioneer the gravel. Where dryas has started forming mats, Savannah sparrows and least sandpipers nest. In alder and willow thickets, hatchlings of orange-crown warblers, fox sparrows, and even occasional hermit thrushes and Oregon juncos harass parents to supply what must seem like endless food. Feathers and flight muscles are made of mosquitoes, blackflies, midges, plant lice, and water beetles.

Glacier Bay's bird list boasts more than 200 entries. Included are species more typical of Arctic tundras and Aleutian grasslands than of southeast Alaska. They are here because of the glaciers. As vegetation sequences progress to the hemlock stage, these birds of the barrens largely forsake the park, replaced by forest species. On the Bartlett Cove trails you hear the plaintive, minor call of varied thrushes and the musical notes of Swainson's and hermit thrushes, birds common throughout Northwest rain forests. Robins are present, their singing—to my ear—like that of a cheerful amateur determined to learn to carry a tune. Kinglets and siskins flit through tree tops in loose, lisping flocks. Three-toed woodpeckers and blue grouse sound their territorial claims, the woodpecker by pounding a dead tree, the grouse by releasing air from throat sacs.

Spring and fall migrations bring birds in, out, and through the park in the ebb and flow of an avian tide. Loons by the thousands stream north along the outer coast in spring. Squadrons of northern phalaropes fly low to the sea in early summer, dropping to feed in tide rips. With winter, old squaw ducks and common murres by the tens of thousands arrive in Glacier Bay, much of their food needs supplied by seabottom dwellers. The shore's mingled sea-and-land resources are crucial for birds as well as land mammals.

One misty Reid Inlet morning Louis and I noticed a small dark dot swimming our way from the far shore. At first we supposed it a seabird, then a seal. On it came, purposefully, straight toward our tent. Within minutes we watched a black bear step onto the beach, shake half dry, and amble from view.

Land animals aren't commonly so close to ice but they don't wholly avoid glaciers. In the shrinking wedge of rubble and runoff that separates the Margerie and Grand Pacific Glaciers, hikers have found brown/grizzly bear and lynx tracks. In Johns Hopkins Inlet, Greg once found evidence of a wolf. For a while there were mice close to the glacier front, probably stowaways in campers' gear. Marmots eke out an existence near Reid Inlet's entrance, their shrill whistle a surprise coming from near sea level because these plump woodchuck-cousins are highcountry characters throughout the West. The elevation seems wrong, but the biome is right.

Land mammals face their own problems in moving back to newly ice-free shores and lowlands. They can't come by air, as the first plants do with wind-blown seeds and spores, or as the first insects do, arriving as winged adults or in bird gullets. Mammals must walk or swim. Even for large animals, extensive

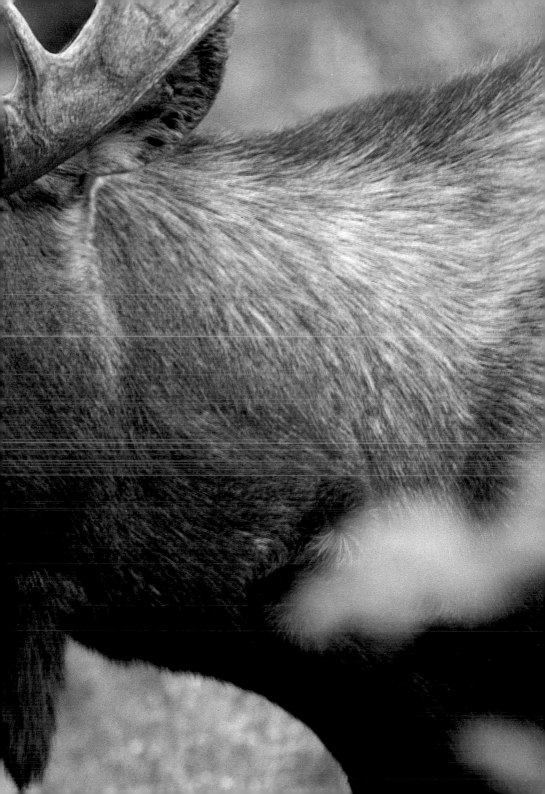

ice or water or mountains may be a formidable barrier.

The two sides of Muir Inlet exemplify the land mammals' disadvantage. Plant succession shows no real difference between sides of the inlet, nor do insect or bird populations. However, the east side hosts several more species than the west. From the east side a low pass connects from Adams Inlet to Lynn Canal and so to the interior. But the west side of Muir Inlet has no such conduit outside. Bounded by ice, mountains, and more saltwater, it is, from the standpoint of life, an island hard to reach.

No true successional stages characterize mammals' pursuit of waning ice. No pioneer species regularly prepare the way for replacements, as with plants. Large mammal firstcomers usually draw on the resources of ecologically young terrain part of the year, moving elsewhere the rest of the year. Gradually, resident populations will build. Moose were first seen in the lowlands east of Muir Inlet in the 1950s, probably having come over Endicott Pass from Lynn Canal. Now you often see moose, or moose sign. Moose have begun to round Tlingit Point into lower Tarr Inlet and have spread throughout the western park, recently to Dundas Bay.

This is also a barrier: mammals haven't had time since the Wisconsinan Ice Age to complete their dispersal throughout southeastern Alaska. The white shroud of the glacial maximum covered most of the region below 600 to 700 meters (2,000 to 2,300 feet) elevation, but it left refugia—green arks of continuing life—north and south of the ice sheet. Brown/grizzly bear, moose, muskrats, and snowshoe hares have repopulated southeastern Alaska from such northern refugia, so far as known. Black bear, wolf, coyote, deer, and mountain goat have come from refugia to the south. Mountain slopes in the Glacier Bay region also provided sky islands of livable habitat for small creatures during the Ice Age. And minor refugia along the park's outer coast escaped getting swallowed by ice during the whole of the Wisconsinan glacier advance. Today 28 mammal species are listed for the park.

Greg Streveler speculates that one or more coastal refugia may have been large enough for the so-called glacier bears to develop as a distinct race of black bears. Their coats took on a distinctive steely blue color. Indians and 19th-century settlers describe these bears as different from black bears and brown/grizzly bears both in looks and behavior. They stayed apart from the other bears, preferring the glacier barrens they probably grew accustomed to during the Ice Age. Glacier bears never became a species of their own, however, and now they've bred back into the black bear population. Even the blue-gray coat appears less and less often.

It's said that only iceworms and glaciologists suffer when the ice sheets disappear. We should add glacier bears to the list. The surest place to see one now is the Juneau Museum.

The Only Constant Is Change

Mountain goats are superbly adapted for scrambling atop rocky crags that would give fits to climbers. Their hooves have cushioned, skidproof pads and their psyches are unflappable. Mountain goats don't panic under pressure; they retreat deliberately, with cool dignity. This pensive critter, on Van Horn Ridge in mid-June, still must shed some winter coat. Those foreleg guard hairs grow 18 centimeters (7 inches) long.

Winter: I came to Glacier Bay in late January once. Perhaps that would be the ideal time for anyone's first trip here. White flakes from white clouds muffle the world. Low peaks seem handsomely tall compared with summer when they're only patched with snow. Spruce and hemlock rim the lower bay as giant, white feather plumes. Up-bay, pan ice skims the water. It gives way with a quiet rasp as your boat cuts through and sends small pieces skittering across the unbroken ice.

The white heads of bald eagles, so conspicuous at other seasons, in winter become camouflage. They look like additional lumps of snow caught on high branches where the birds perch. Occasional blood spots and scattered feathers dot the frozen sea, left from seabirds that became eagle dinners. Cormorants fly low, wings whirring as though the birds were trying to catch up to their own heads. The goldeneye ducks, old-squaws, and murres that have arrived for the winter continually up-end themselves to feed beneath the surface. Seals rise to stare with brown eyes incredibly soft. The seals in winter number only about half the bay's summer population and most now stay away from the ice. Their probable diet is fish, shrimp, and crabs.

That January I traveled up-bay aboard the National Park Service supply boat *Nunatak*, joining a group led by Greg Streveler, to make a winter wildlife census in Adams Inlet. It didn't take long to begin the count. As we motored ashore from *Nunatak* the first morning, a river otter streaked through slabs of pan ice that lay on the lowtide shore like oversized almond bark candy. Above the jumbled slabs we found three crab shells, apparently the otter's dinner midden. Rock sandpipers made a close-packed cluster of 80 to 90 black dots where a river emptied into the inlet. While strapping on skis, I noticed a midge the size and form of a mosquito. It was tiptoeing across the snow, wings held straight up over its back.

Such insects are suited to winter because they spend most of their lives as aquatic larvae and need only a day or so out of water to mate and lay eggs and die. For that bit of time they can cope with almost any weather. Spiders also stalked the snow as we set off. They apparently have a built-in antifreeze to pump through their veins. Soon after striding out on our skis we heard the birdlike trill of a red squirrel, a species that arrived in the park via Endicott Gap only within the last decade or two.

Our plan was to check for animal tracks along beaches, creeks, and at the junctions between slopes and adjoining flats, chief winter routes of animals. Fresh snow skimmed a firm crust. Mountains rimmed a white world. Brown traceries of alder and cottonwood branches rose out of snow perhaps 40 centimeters (16 inches) deep.

Wolverine tracks laced the edge of a thicket—hiding place for ptarmigan—and farther on we spotted the wolverine loping along the beach. Wolf tracks were frequent. We found one shallow depression in the snow where a lone wolf had rested, protected from wind by a low bank. Greg guessed it came a long distance or it wouldn't have lain down. This wasn't a bedding ground because no urine yellowed the snow. Out on the flat three sets of tracks overlapped and braided as they followed the river bank. Turning onto a high moraine, they vanished in the alder. All the wolf scat we found held mountain goat hair.

Seven winters before, Greg counted more than 200 goats in the Adams Inlet area. We saw none. Summer cruise ship passengers back then almost always saw them as white dots in alpine meadows, particularly on Mount Wright. Not so now. Two successive winters of deep snow brought trouble for the animals. Browse was buried. Even beach salt grass and sedge were covered. Getting around was equally troublesome, because sharp hooves and deep snow make a poor combination.

Wolves found the severe conditions less crucially difficult. Their broad feet upholstered with stiff hair facilitate snow travel. And potential food for the wolves was ample that winter because the mountain goats were conveniently forced down to the shore. Predators don't, as biologists formerly believed, necessarily rely exclusively on weak animals. In this case the wolves might take animals in any state of health, eating only choice parts—there's more where that came from. Predator numbers go up; prey numbers drop. Then the pendulum swings and predator numbers drop, maintaining balance over time. Populations and species seem to be what matter, not individuals.

Aboard *Ginjur*: My journal from the research boat *Ginjur* notes that "Charles Jurasz greeted Austin Post saying, 'You're the bottom man and I'm the whale man.' Biologist and glaciologist then disappeared into the wheelhouse to pencil notations onto marine charts." The *Ginjur* is a converted 15-meter (50-foot) Navy ship-to-shore transport aboard which biologist-owner Chuck Jurasz is researching acoustics, which is why he wanted *Growler's* depth information for Glacier Bay's underwater basins. Additional work will show details: where is the bottom soft and sound-absorbing and where does bare bedrock reflect sound back into the water, perhaps echoing it, or—for a whale—accentuating it painfully?

Beyond *Ginjur's* fantail I watched chunky little murrelets flip themselves below the surface, then bob back up, each with a silver fish dangling from its bill. Humpback whales also feed on these capelin. 45-ton monarchs swallowing 84-gram (3-ounce) prey. Humpbacks sometimes lunge to the surface with their mouths agape, scooping in a ton of water and capelin or krill, and opening out their accordian-pleated undersides. Powerful throat muscles then force the water through curtains of baleen, catching prey as though in a sieve. The pleats fold shut.

Chuck has seen three whales working together, rising with the dark sides of their flippers uppermost, only to suddenly turn them over, flashing the white undersides. Perhaps the light color of the humpbacks' extraordinary flippers, far longer than those of any other whale, helps to concentrate the feed. He has also watched the whales flick their great tails forward, whooshing the chowderlike water toward their open mouths. Chuck has seen this scores of times but— and this he emphasizes—only by two individuals: Garfunkle and Gertrude.

"Garf is innovative," says Chuck, who recognizes these individuals by the distinctive color patterns of flippers and flukes. "Garf's always coming up with something the other whales aren't doing. He started

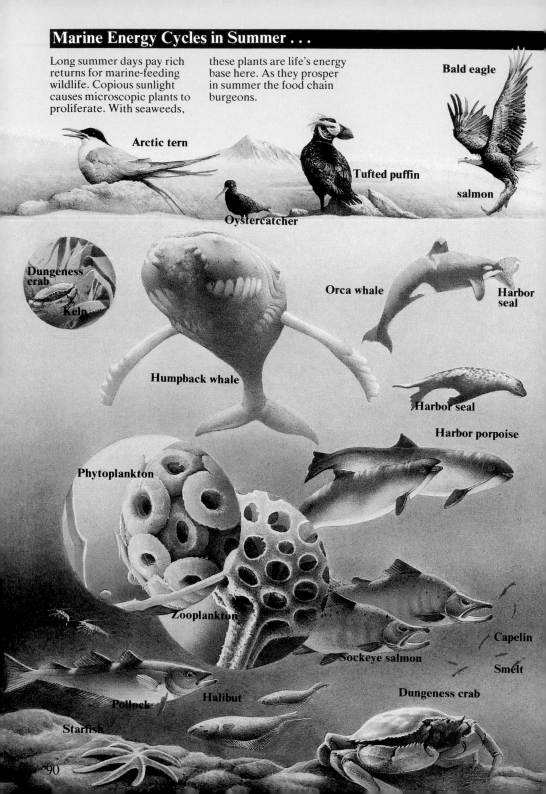

Marine Energy Cycles in Summer . . .

Long summer days pay rich returns for marine-feeding wildlife. Copious sunlight causes microscopic plants to proliferate. With seaweeds, these plants are life's energy base here. As they prosper in summer the food chain burgeons.

Bald eagle

Arctic tern

Tufted puffin

salmon

Oystercatcher

Dungeness crab

Kelp

Orca whale

Harbor seal

Humpback whale

Harbor seal

Harbor porpoise

Phytoplankton

Zooplankton

Sockeye salmon

Capelin

Smelt

Dungeness crab

Pollock

Halibut

Starfish

And in Winter

Marine life grows sparse in winter as pan ice, increased salinity, and short days stifle plant production. Only bottom feeders and marine creatures that live off body reserves boast year-round populations. These suffice to support some waterfowl over winter.

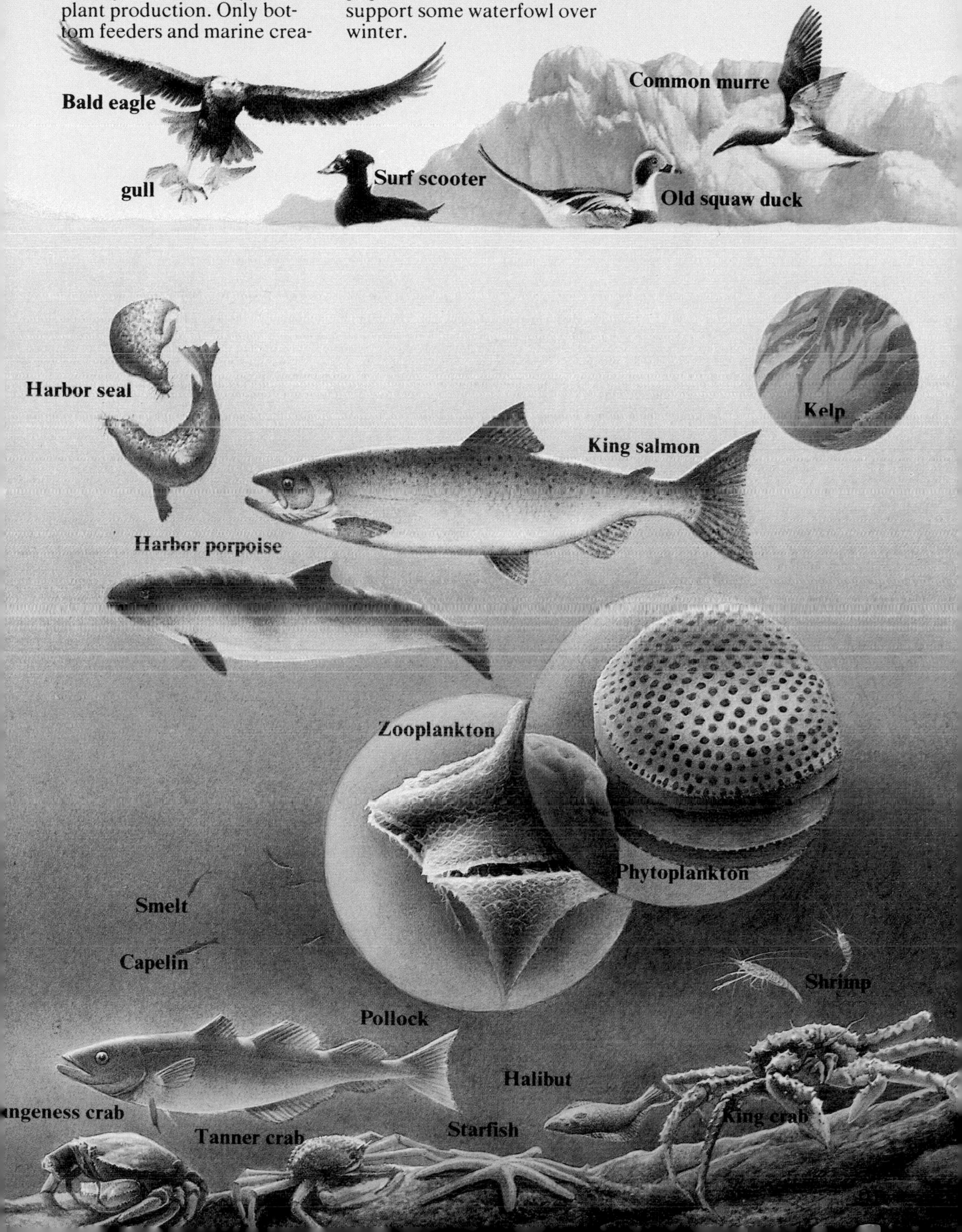

Common murre

Bald eagle

gull

Surf scooter

Old squaw duck

Harbor seal

Kelp

King salmon

Harbor porpoise

Zooplankton

Phytoplankton

Smelt

Capelin

Shrimp

Pollock

Halibut

ngeness crab

Tanner crab

Starfish

King crab

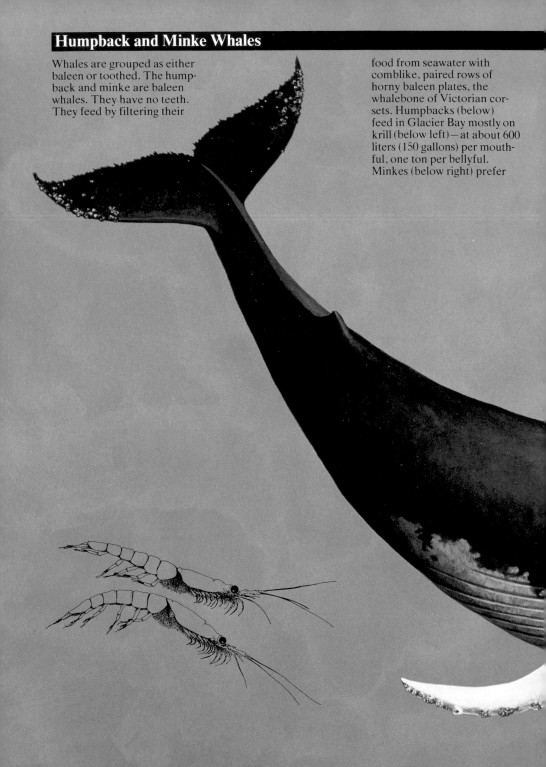

Humpback and Minke Whales

Whales are grouped as either baleen or toothed. The humpback and minke are baleen whales. They have no teeth. They feed by filtering their food from seawater with comblike, paired rows of horny baleen plates, the whalebone of Victorian corsets. Humpbacks (below) feed in Glacier Bay mostly on krill (below left)—at about 600 liters (150 gallons) per mouthful, one ton per bellyful. Minkes (below right) prefer

fish in these waters. Adult humpbacks average 12 to 15 meters (40 to 50 feet) long and weigh about 2.5 tons per meter (about three quarters of a ton per foot). Decimated by whaling, these coast-loving creatures are now protected under the Endangered Species Act and international agreements. Minke whales grow to about 10 meters (33 feet) in northern waters. Among the large whales they are fast swimmers, making up to 32 kilometers per hour (20 mph). Minkes are now the most heavily harvested baleen whales, since taking others has been restricted.

The Orca (or Killer) Whale

Orca whales are also known as killer whales. These toothed whales can hunt in packs, called pods, and have been dubbed wolves of the sea. They eat fish, sea lions, seals, porpoises, sharks, squid, and other whales. Orcas have even killed blue whales, the largest creatures—at 100 tons, or the weight of about 2,250 men—that the world has ever known. Orca adults average about 7 meters (23 feet) long and can sustain speeds up to 45 kilometers per hour (29 mph). The largely triangular dorsal fin may reach nearly 2 meters (6 feet) high on old males. Its prominence and their black-and-white markings on belly, flanks, and head make the orca unmistakable. Orcas eat a staggering variety of marine animals, including warm-blooded species. The range of foods available to them is greatly enhanced by their diving ability. Orcas can dive to nearly 1,000 meters (3,400 feet); Glacier Bay isn't that deep, however. When whales dive, blood is forced from their muscles into the brain and the buildup of carbon dioxide in their lungs does not force them to breathe, as it would humans. Killer-whale attacks on boats are both rare and largely undocumented. One killing—unsubstantiated—of a fisherman off Baja California was reported in 1977. The orca's rapacity is exaggerated in whaling literature from unscientific samplings of one specimen's stomach contents. Docile in captivity and keenly intelligent, orca whales are star aquarium performers.

feeding this way one summer off Johns Hopkins and the next year, while following him, Gertrude began doing it too."

Bubble-net feeding? Chuck first noted this in 1968. He saw bubbles rising in a ring where he knew a submerged whale was. "Hey, it's letting out air underwater instead of at the surface," he thought. Then he saw the water come alive with herring and the whale rising through the fish, jaws open. The whale was working like men do in a hatchery, using bubbles to shunt fish to where they're wanted. The bubble net nicely concentrated the capelin in position to swallow! All previous whale records—s.f.a.k.—mention this feeding method only once. This is in a French report written years ago by a Norwegian whaler in the Antarctic.

The paucity of written records is a problem. "We know about whales from chasing and killing them," Chuck explains. "You can read a lot about anatomy and the measurements taken from carcasses. But until very recently you couldn't read much about the living animals. What we're getting aboard *Ginjur* is basic data on how humpbacks feed in Alaska: what they go after, how they capture it, and where they have to go to find it."

From the late 1960s to '70s, 20 to 24 humpbacks summered in Glacier Bay. But in 1978 and continuing into the '80s, fewer whales seem to have come. Why? Despite research, nobody knows.

Investigators find that an enormous quantity of humpback food is available in Glacier Bay waters, but it quite likely varies at times. Also, park waters may be somewhat noisier than those nearby.

Noise from ship engines and small boat motors seems more noticeable here than nearby, and vessel traffic here is greater.

Understanding has barely begun. Consequently, park regulations require staying at least 400 meters (0.25 mile) away from whales; and courses for water travel may at times be restricted. Today's humpback whales have few havens. Extinction threatens—and extinction lasts forever.

Disrupted balances inevitably domino. Take sea otters as an example. Lapérouse, remarking on their beauty and abundance along Glacier Bay's outer coast, estimated that a Lituya Bay factory could take 10,000 skins per year from the coast. Only a few years after Lapérouse's visit, a Russian vessel arrived bringing Aleut hunters and 450 of their *bidarkas*, fleet skin boats much like Eskimo kayaks. Within mere days, men stowed 1,800 sea otter skins into the ship's hold. Most were from the Aleuts' kills, but many were from trade with resident Tlingits. Lituya Bay was a prime sea otter hunting ground.

Sea otters were killed off along this coast by the dawn of the 20th century, and the effects of such a loss are only now beginning to be understood. The entire marine community is involved, not necessarily negatively but with repercussions of implicit change. Sea otters feed on sea urchins, which in turn feed on kelp. Eliminate the otters and urchins increase, eating far more kelp. A plethora of plants and animals next are affected, because kelp beds are the great nearshore nurseries of many ocean species. Eventually seabirds, eagles, seals, bears, and even people are bound to feel the change.

Dundas Bay, aboard *Taku*: Rain during the night. *Taku* bobbed considerably, especially at the turn of the tide. Yesterday we went ashore to explore, wearing every bit of rain gear we possess. Today will be the same. Checking the long abandoned salmon cannery here in Dundas Bay, we found the pilings deeply worn at the base, etched by saltwater and time. Some have fallen. Those still standing look like trees gnawed by a beaver. Remarkably, two big brick-walled boilers remain in place on the pilings, though they surely can't stay perched much longer. Nearby, timbers mark what once was a shipway, and a wrecked barge lies stranded at the hightide line.

Near the forest edge is a cabin with a sign reading "Government Property." The door is unlocked but a note asks you to close the cabin carefully when leaving, to keep out mice. Inside, there's an oil-barrel stove and a pencilled invitation to "Have a warm time." Old magazines include *Quest* with an article on whale watching promoted on the cover but missing inside. A guest log requests "Please sign in," but names from the last five years take up less than a page. Earlier pages have been torn out. A note addressed "Dear *Nunatak*" and dated three years ago asks that the cabin's mattress be taken to Bartlett Cove. The mattress still is here.

Dave Bohn writes in *Glacier Bay, the Land and the Silence* that this cannery started in 1898. Sixty-

Tlingit Indians

Tlingit Indians living in Hoonah, a village diagonally across Icy Strait from Glacier Bay, have proud family songs and stories about advancing ice that drove their ancestors from *Tcukanedi*, the Valley of the River of Grass. This was probably on former shorelines in lower Glacier Bay. There stood a village. And there a young girl, ritually confined during her first menses, violated cultural dictates and in her loneliness called to glaciers on the slope above. Her cries brought them down. Ice over-rode the people's lands and waters. It obliterated the seal hunting grounds and the meadows and muskegs rich with berries and fleshy roots. It covered the streams ideal for summer and fall salmon fishing. Gone were the beaches and sea cliffs where

the spring egg gathering was so easy that Tlingits today still speak of "picking" eggs, not hunting them. The Tlingit Clan fled first to the Home Shore, east of today's Excursion Inlet. Then in time they fled across Icy Strait to Hoonah. It was the Little Ice Age glacier advance that had driven these peoples from Glacier Bay. Before their ancestral shores had melted free again, their aboriginal days collided with the arrival of Europeans, and life began a new and radically different era.

Joe and Muz Ibach (above) built their cabin (left) in the 1920s at Reid Inlet. Their gold operations, supplemented with gardening and foraging, kept them alive, but that's all. Some years they went in the hole for freight and processing. One year they netted $13.

one men worked here, half of them Chinese, the others Caucasian and Tlingit fishermen who supplied salmon. A 1912 photo shows about 40 houses along the beach north of the cabin. Now none is discernible.

From our anchorage we have two objectives ashore: Buck Harbeson's place and the old Tlingit cemetery up the river. Harbeson, a prospector, died here in 1964 alone in his cabin. He had come 33 years earlier to work on Doc Silvers' claim. Silvers had arrived with his wife in 1928. The rain and the silence of our few days in Dundas Bay were theirs year-round, although canneries, salteries (the predecessors of canneries), small mines, and fox farms then accounted for a human population here far greater than today's. A farflung neighborliness must have prevailed as an antidote for the cabin's poignant isolation or, perhaps, as an irritant for any hardcore recluse. Before the arrival of miners and cannery men, fox farmers and squatters, the Tlingits lived here.

The remnants of Harbeson's cabin remind me of Reid Inlet and the Ibachs' little barn-red cabin. When Louis and I stayed there squares of wallpaper samples covered the walls of the Ibachs' back room. Halves of a Mother's Day card were tacked over the two bunks, the cover picture—roses—above one bunk, the inside message over the other. Dave Bohn's book includes a snapshot of the Ibachs (above). They have that gentle expression frequent among people living alone in the wilds. You expect a grizzled, weary, hard look. Instead there's this incredible innocence. Jim Huscroft had that look. He raised foxes on Cenotaph Island in Lituya Bay from around World War I until his death, alone, in 1939.

The 1936 Lituya Bay wave damaged Huscroft's cabin. The 1958 wave demolished it. Pieces of stovewood and scraps of plumbing scattered through the alder are all that tell of its presence now. Human marks have never been great in this country.

Gales today are reported on the outer coast. Winds to 60 knots and 4.5-meter (15-foot) seas. Louis is ashore with the water cans at a stream that flows over granite boulders in an idyllic, mossy, rain-forest setting. Chess stands in the cockpit fishing. We've decided against going ashore to look for the Harbeson cabin. Nor will we chance taking the

Jim Huscroft raised foxes on Cenotaph Island in Lituya Bay from about World War I until he died there alone in 1939. The 1958 wave in Lituya Bay wiped out his cabin.

dinghy up-river to the Tlingit cemetery. This anchorage is too poor and too windy for all of us to leave *Taku*. We thought about holing up and waiting, but have decided to head out.

Gray sky, gray sea. The shore shows only as a low blue-black streak. No mountains, no detail. We failed to explore either cabin or cemetery but the day's mood and the unseen traces of humanity beyond the porthole now merge into remembrance of having once rowed to a grave island opposite today's Tlingit village of Hoonah. You walk across the beach there, climb a bank, and step into the dripping hemlock forest. Headstones are decorated with marble cherubs and crosses that include Russian Orthodox crosses with a second, dipped crossbar. Indian clan crests mingle with the Christian symbols. A marble grizzly drapes over one headstone. A wolf head tops another, jaws open, teeth and tongue realistically carved. There are marble salmon, dogfish, eagles, ravens, and a stone chief's hat embellished with a wolf's face which is outlined with abalone shell.

Step among such graves and you feel a shiver of time and of intersecting cultures. Talk with Indian villagers and you feel it even more. The mother of one of our Hoonah friends watched the Russian flag come down and the 35-star American flag go up in 1865 at Sitka. The entire English-speaking era in Alaska spans just two generations.

Go further back in human time and you come to the tale of ice forcing the *Tcukanedi* people out of Glacier Bay. Further still, and you're reading archeology reports. Near Point Couverden—where I found the best huckleberry picking of my life—Dr. Robert Ackerman of Washington State University excavated a site that radiocarbon dates as 10,000 years old. The Ground Hog Bay site is one of only two comparably old sites known so far in Alaska. The other is on nearby Admiralty Island.

Bits of charcoal give the date. With them lay stone choppers, gravers, scrapers, and tiny blades technically called microblades, significant because they represent a distinct, and sophisticated, tool manufacturing technique found on both the Russian and American sides of Bering Strait. A paint stone was also found at Ground Hog Bay: part of a woman's cosmetic kit? a shaman's medicine kit? the palette an artist used in painting hide?

The Ground Hog Bay site now stands 13.3 meters (44 feet) above sea level, or it did in 1965 when Ackerman and his crew first tested their discovery. Now it must be minutely higher, rebounding as the ice continues to retreat. When the fires of early peoples flickered there the site was at beach level, for artifacts and charcoal lay in beach gravel. Beneath the beach gravel are glacial deposits. Layers of time.

Taku's voyage is ending. Two porpoises are close off the starboard bow. A distant storm petrel flies low to the water, utterly controlled. We're heading for Elfin Cove and from there to Juneau to reboard the ferry. Are we returning to reality or are we leaving it?

Part 3

Guide and Adviser

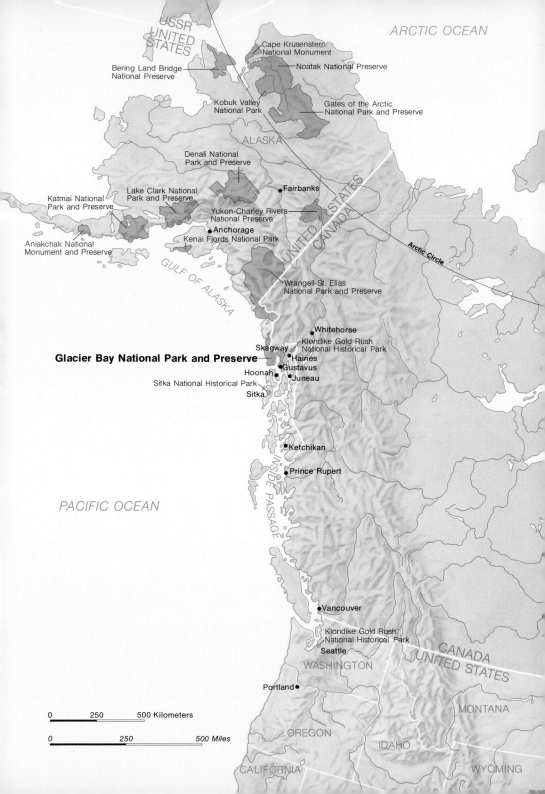

Getting to Glacier Bay

Glacier Bay National Park and Preserve lies west of Juneau and can be reached only by plane or boat. The only road just connects Gustavus and its airfield to park headquarters at Bartlett Cove (11 kilometers/7 miles). There is no link with the Alaska highway system.

Alaska Airlines provides daily jet service from Juneau to Gustavus (about 30 minutes) in the summer season, which runs from mid-May to mid-September. Passengers are transported between Gustavus and Bartlett Cove — at flight time only — by bus-limo. Year-round air service to Gustavus is available by small plane but no regular off-season ground transportation runs between Gustavus and the park. Scenic flights, charters, and air taxi service — including floatplane service — are offered in summer by a concessioner at Glacier Bay Lodge, and year-round out of Gustavus, Hoonah, and Juneau. Write the superintendent for a list of operators.

By Boat or Ship Limited tour boat service from Juneau to Glacier Bay is usually available from May until early fall, but you must inquire before making plans. Charter boat arrangements are sometimes possible out of Juneau or Gustavus. Write the Juneau Chamber of Commerce. Private boats are welcome, but write ahead to the superintendent for special regulations. (For boat service at Glacier Bay see Trips Up the Bay.)

Write the superintendent for a list of ship companies that offer Alaska cruises featuring a day in Glacier Bay. On such cruises you will want sun, wind, and rain protection gear so that you can enjoy being on deck. You'll want binoculars for both scenery and wildlife.

Topical Reference

Address for Information:
Superintendent, Glacier Bay National Park and Preserve, Gustavus, AK 99826

Pages 104-105: *At 1:30 a.m. on May 23 at this campsite on Brady Glacier, only the tent fabric glows warm red.*

Pages 108-109: *Some management regulations for the preserve area — at upper left on your map — may differ from those normally associated with National Park Service areas. For information check with a ranger or write the superintendent.*

YAKUTAT
GLACIER

NOVATAK GLACIER

Alsek River

BRITISH COLUMBIA

SAINT

ALSEK RANGE

MELBURN GLACIER

Tatshenshini River

Alsek River

Dry Bay

Airstrip
Cabin

East Alsek
River

NATIONAL
PRESERVE

Alsek Glacier

Grand Plateau
Glacier

ELIAS

MOUNTAINS

GRAND

PACIFIC

GLACIER

CANADA
UNITED STATES

1966

Mt. Lodge
3210
10,530

Mt. Root
3859
12,660

Mt. Fairweather
4670
15,300

Mt. Quincy Adams
4161
13,650

F
A
I
R
W
E
A
T
H
E
R

R
A
N
G
E

Mt. Salisbury
3658
12,000

1966

Johns Hopkins

Co

Fairweather Glacier

Cape
Fairweather

Lituya Mountain
3582
11,750

Johns Hopkins Glacier

1929

Mt. Abbe
2667
8750

N A T I O N A

Mt.
Bertha
3048
10,000

Lituya Bay

Mt. Crillon
3879
12,728

PACIFIC OCEAN

GULF OF
ALASKA

LaPerouse Glacier

Mt. LaPerou
3270
10,728

Icy Point

North

↑

0   5   10 Kilometers

0   5   10 Miles

Glacier Bay
National Park

Glacier Bay
National Preserve

Trail

1966

Historic extent of
glaciation

1564
5138

Elevations are shown in
meters, with feet in *Italics*.

Weather and Seasons

This is a land of glaciers. Clouds make and perpetuate glaciers, so, for weeks at a stretch, "good" weather may mean a day of only scant rain. Clear days rate as blue-sky days and most agree such weather is best. But don't despair on gray days. Distant views are blocked, but mist hangs wraith-like above the water, first swaddling, then releasing, nearby peaks. The bay seems to brood, mysterious. Gray days are typical, although rain usually is light and intermittent. May and June usually bring the most sunshine and the least rain, but never trust statistics here. The visitor season runs from mid-May through mid-September.

Generally, weather runs cool in summer and surprisingly mild in winter, with abundant rainfall all year. Rainfall generally increases as the summer progresses into early fall. Bring clothing for possible below-freezing temperatures, no matter the month. Carry full rain protection—for head, torso, legs, and feet—even aboardship, so you can be on deck in all weather.

"Layer" your clothing: Several lightweight shirts and sweaters worn under a windproof, rainproof parka or jacket offer a range of temperature readiness while you're outdoors. Attend to protecting wrists, throat, and head against heat loss with cap, high turtlenecks, and sleeve cuffs. (Hikers and kayakers please read clothing and gear advice under Enjoying the Backcountry.) The maritime climate moderates and mutes differences in the change of seasons. In April bears come out of hibernation. Waterfowl begin coming through. Seabirds arrive to nest and hummingbirds return. Seals give birth beginning in late May. The first whales usually arrive at Bartlett Cove in late June, to begin gorging on the krill—tons of krill—that will sustain them, as stored fat, through the winter.

Waves of color along the shore tell you what's happening to the calendar. Green leaves burst from lowland willow and alder in May. Alpine meadows turn green in July. Fireweed blossoms paint the upper beach rose-purple from July to mid-August. By late August, cottonwoods glow golden. In late summer and early fall the snow is gone from the ridges and low peaks. Berries ripen in abundance and the salmon make their migrations into the rivers. The whales and summer birds begin to leave. During starry nights the aurora borealis—northern lights—appear.

Insects, Insects, Insects Alaska is notorious for the ferocity of its biting insects. Gnats and flies are worse than mosquitoes here. Aboardship you'll probably not be troubled. But ashore ... you may see mountain goats with their muzzles buried in snow to escape getting bitten. Or you may see a cloud of insects encircling a bear.

Higher country is generally worse for bugs than the low country. Some years are plain awful—mosquitoes, deerflies, horseflies, white sox, and no-see-ums are all out for blood. Most years aren't that bad. But bring insect repellent and adequate screening for your tent. Beaches often have enough breeze to hold biting insects to a minimum. Bushes can fairly swarm with them. (Mosquitoes subsist on plant juices if they have to.)

Backpackers hike along a crevasse, a deep fissure in the ice, on Geikie Glacier in mid-August. This former tidewater glacier has retreated high above its inlet on the bay's west shore.

Naturalist Programs

Park naturalists lead hikes daily in summer from the lodge and they board cruise ships and tour boats to answer your questions and interpret the scenery and wildlife. Exhibits housed in the lodge portray the park's glacier story, the return of life as ice retreats, and the marine energy cycle. Exhibits on the dock treat whales and marine life. At the Gustavus airfield terminal an exhibit introduces Southeastern Alaska and summarizes the Glacier Bay ecology.

Up-bay, rangers are stationed at Goose Cove in the summer. Look for their white tents floating offshore on platforms (for protection from bears). Rangers offer information, and help in emergencies. Similar summer ranger stations usually operate intermittently on Cenotaph Island in Lituya Bay, and at Graves Harbor or Dundas Bay.

Films about Glacier Bay are shown daily in summer at the lodge. Naturalists give slide-illustrated talks in the evenings. Schedules are posted in the lodge.

A naturalist meets the bus that brings jet passengers from the airport to Bartlett Cove. The naturalist offers a camper orientation talk and will suggest the best areas to visit during your stay. You will also receive safety information and have ample opportunity to ask any questions you may have.

Various publications are available. They deal with such topics as the humpback whales, bear safety, and intertidal life at Bartlett Cove. The free park newspaper tells you where to get information about the day's events, and provides general Glacier Bay information, including safety precautions and important management regulations.

Accommodations and Services

Glacier Bay Lodge, a concession, operates from about mid-May to mid-September. It is the only hostelry in the park. Rooms are motel-style. The central unit offers lobby, dining room, bar, auditorium, and exhibits about the park. Make room reservations well in advance. Full meal and bar services and the free park naturalist programs are open to all, not just to lodge guests. For information and reservations write: Glacier Bay Lodge, Glacier Bay National Park, Gustavus, AK 99826 during the operating season, or Glacier Bay Lodge, Inc., 312 Park Place Bldg., Seattle, WA 98101 the rest of the year.

A family-operated hotel in Gustavus offers rooms and meals.

Campground The National Park Service maintains a forest campground near the lodge at Bartlett Cove (no reservation or fees required). Facilities include a bearproof food cache, fire pits, and firewood. Campground stays are limited to 14 days maximum. Bring all equipment and supplies. Gustavus has only one small general store and grocery. Juneau is the nearest full-supply point. Glacier Bay Lodge usually sells white gas, but no other campstove fuels. Pets must be leashed in the campground and are prohibited in the backcountry. There is no place to store extra gear—at campground, lodge, or park headquarters—while you are in the backcountry.

Bartlett Cove Concession A dock facility at Bartlett Cove sells No. 2 diesel fuel and gasoline for boats. Tie-up space is not available except for fueling, though anchorage is good and unrestricted. No buoys. A tidal grid facilitates hull inspection and repair. Limited snack-type groceries are sold at the lodge. The lodge's showers, laundromat, public phone, dining room, bar, and gift shop are open to all, not just to lodge guests.

Bartlett Cove Activities Be sure to take in the daily naturalist programs at the lodge. Schedules are posted in the lobby. You can also hike the trails. A short trail leads through the forest and along the beach to the dock. The other trail meanders by a tidal lagoon and into the forest to the Bartlett River estuary (12 kilometers/8 miles round trip). River fishing can be pretty good in July for cutthroat and Dolly Varden trout. In May and June birdsong is everywhere, as bird migrations are at their peak. In June and July the forest and beach flowers bloom. August brings the onset of fall colors, not spectacular here, and the ripening of berries, which are spectacular. Take your pick of strawberries, blueberries, huckleberries, nagoon berries, and several others. In late summer you can watch salmon enter the Bartlett River to spawn. This is one of the world's great nature sights. Ducks, geese, and other waterfowl concentrate in the lagoon for fall migration. Coyotes forage the beach year-round.

Fishing An Alaska fishing license is required in the park. Licenses are sold in Juneau, at the Gustavus Post Office, at Glacier Bay Lodge, or by mail. You can arrange charter boat and fishing guide services at the Glacier Bay Lodge. Halibut and salmon are the chief sport fish. The lodge chef will prepare your catch for your dinner that evening, or you can arrange to send frozen fish home via Alaska Airlines. Up-bay, crab and shrimp pots are worth a try. Some freshwater streams and lakes harbor Dolly Varden and cutthroat trout. Consult a ranger about your angling itinerary.

Margerie Glacier's ice front (top) looms high above the serene waters of Tarr Inlet. In a boat this big, this may be as close as you can get to Canada—see map—only to be stopped short by ice, the Grand Pacific Glacier.

Strawberries thrive in this moist, marine climate, and they are not averse to disturbed land and sandy soils.

113

Trips Up the Bay

You should plan on an excursion up-bay. The nearest tidewater glacier is about 70 kilometers (43 miles) from Bartlett Cove. Cruise ships generally spend a leisurely day traveling to at least one glacier front so passengers can watch the birth of icebergs. A concessioner-operated tour boat departs the lodge every morning for a six- to eight-hour trip up the bay, giving a look at icebergs, glaciers, and wildlife. Park naturalists accompany both cruise ships and the tour boat. The concessioner offers overnight boat trips in summer, although they are often heavily booked. Inquire way ahead, if possible.

Backcountry hikers, campers, kayakers, and canoeists are let off the tour boat and picked up again at designated points up-bay. The cost is based on the regular tour boat fee with added drop-off or pickup charges. Make advance arrangements. Only about five drop-offs and pickups are feasible per day. Floatplane taxi service often can be arranged, but check first about transporting rigid kayaks, etc. The only alternative to boat or plane transport is a long paddle up-bay. Hiking to the upper bay from Bartlett Cove is not practical.

You can often arrange air or boat taxi service out of Juneau, Gustavus, or Hoonah. Guided kayak trips are offered out of Gustavus. Write for current information.

Whale and Seal Watching Comparatively few people have ever seen a whale in the wild. And while nobody guarantees you'll see humpback whales, chances are good in June, July, and August. Please remember that the whales need peace more than you need a close look. Don't pursue whales. Let binoculars and long lenses close the gap. Minke whales occasionally enter Glacier Bay. So do orcas (killer whales) and harbor porpoises. Boaters mostly see the humpback whales, which usually just flash their arched backs capped with a small fin. Occasionally, however, humpbacks display their full, prodigious dimensions in leaps from the water ("breaching"). Whales react to approaching boats in various ways. They sometimes slap the water with their side flippers ("finning") or with their flukes ("tail lobbing"). Humpbacks may also react simply by moving away from the boat or even abandoning the area. The North Pacific Ocean population of humpback whales has been reduced to about 850 individuals by commerical whaling. They are now so scarce worldwide that they are protected under the Federal Endangered Species Act. They arrive here from their calving grounds near Baja, California and Hawaii with a purpose: to eat enough to store the fat to see them through the winter. Humpbacks do not feed year round.

Glacier Bay's harbor porpoises are considered one of the world's few untrammeled populations. More than a hundred have been counted feeding together in Sitakaday Narrows where riptides bring nutrient-rich bottom water to the surface. You may see Dall porpoises in Icy Strait playing in your vessel's bow wake. Hair seals are seen almost anywhere in Glacier Bay waters. Great throngs ride the pack ice of upper, tidewater-glacier inlets during the early-summer pupping season. Don't approach them during mid-May to mid-June, the crucial weeks of mother-pup bond formation. Disturbance may cause a mother to permanently abandon her young. Certain death ensues for the hapless pup.

Enjoying the Backcountry

Plan carefully so you are well supplied but not overburdened with gear. You will meet wilderness on its terms, not yours. Count on rain: May and June average the least, August and September grow steadily wetter. Most years, snow lingers well into June in the low country and blankets alpine ridges and meadows into July or even August. Snow may fall, even at sea level, any month, but is unlikely down low from mid-June through September.

Bring waterproof clothing, a tent with waterproof fly, a rain cover for your pack, waterproof matches, and waterproof food bags. If you're kayaking, add a spray cover. Then still expect to be wet part of the time anyway. Wool clothing is advisable because it retains warmth while wet. Cotton and most synthetics do not. However, synthetic-fill sleeping bags and jackets retain much insulative quality even when soggy, and they can be wrung half dry. By contrast, down bags and clothing lose all insulation value when wet. Guard down garments zealously during wet conditions. And remember that the wet from sweat is just as wet—and chilling—as rain.

Some hikers favor ponchos rather than rain pants and parka because their built-in ventilation prevents overheating. But wind whipping a poncho out of control may discount its rain protection too. New, one-way permeable rain gear is designed to solve this problem, but opinions vary on its effectiveness. In fact, no two backpackers or kayakers are likely to agree on the best solution to the wet-within-versus-wet-without dilemma. In summary, be sure that you're equipped either with clothing that stays warm while wet or with clothing carefully kept dry until needed and feasible to wear. Hypothermia—critical loss of

Kayakers prepare to leave the mother ship for paddling and backpacking near Riggs Glacier, far up Muir Inlet. They and their kayak booked passage up the bay on the tour boat Thunder Bay.

body heat—is serious and can strike any time of year. Hypothermia can cause death, even when the temperature is well above freezing.

While you must be prepared for wet and cold, you should also bring lightweight clothing, in case of hot weather, and plenty of sunburn preventative.

Extensive hiking, especially under pack, requires sturdy boots. Rubber boots or tennis shoes won't do. (Boat boots, however, are a blessing for getting in and out of kayaks or other small craft.) Carry moleskin or sponge rubber tape, even if you're not prone to blisters. Wet feet can develop sore spots. Apply tape at the *first* hint of trouble. If you think caring for a barely begun blister is annoying, just wait until it's beyond the stage at which simple taping can help!

A sleeping pad or air mattress will afford comfort and insulate you against the cold ground. A mosquito net for your tent is a must. You need fine mesh, to keep out gnats; or try a double layer of netting as defense.

Where to Go?   There are no trails in Glacier Bay National Park and Preserve except at Bartlett Cove. Carry a compass and topographic map—maps are sold at the lodge or by mail—and know how to use them *before* you begin your trip. Don't travel alone, and let a ranger know your itinerary and expected return. Be prepared for steep, rocky slopes, maddening tangles of alder and devil's club, vast barrens, rivers that can rise treacherously in heavy rain, and rivers that become torrents on hot afternoons when ice melt is greatest. Also expect beauty that will stretch your soul and haunt you forever.

To be close to tidewater ice, go to upper Muir Inlet on the bay's east side,

or Reid, Johns Hopkins, or Tarr Inlets on the west side. Lituya Bay and the LaPerouse Glacier, on the outer coast, are also close to ice, but approach by air taxi is all but required. For stagnant remnants of once-mighty Little Ice Age glaciers, check Muir Inlet maps. Brown with mineral overburden and safe to approach, such ice once characterized much of northern North America. Ask a ranger about the current ice condition, however. Glacier retreat is so rapid that even recent maps may show ice where none now exists.

Forest Creek, off lower Muir Inlet, boasts fossil trees still standing upright as they are exposed by erosion in gravel banks. A ranger can mark your map for other fossil tree locations.

Delightful coves, inlets, and islands offering wildlife and plants in varying stages of colonization are available by the score as destinations, many with valleys or slopes that lead to high ridges and over into adjoining drainages. Put a pin on the map while blindfolded and you'll probably pick well! But to fit interest and energies to available time and experience, you'll do best to talk over options with a park ranger. And read the Trips Up the Bay section about backcountry access and transport. An excellent hiking guide for Muir Inlet is sold by the Alaska Natural History Association, upstairs at the lodge, or by mail (See Armchair Explorations).

Making Your Camp   Avoid camping on beaches bordered by bluffs or plant thickets where animals—from mountain goats to wolverines, coyotes, wolves, and bears—have their established thoroughfares. Also respect the territory of nesting birds. Both North and South Marble Islands, and other islands, are closed to camping, or even to going ashore, from May 1 to September 1. This is to protect nesting birds. Ask a park ranger about any other restrictions on camp locations. Naturally disturbed places, such as outwash areas, are recommended as campsites. Stay *well* above high tide line, preferably above the ryegrass zone.

Firewood is not available in the upper bay. The only wood there is fossil wood, hundreds of thousands of years old, killed by previous glaciations. This wood should not be burned. Bring a stove and fuel bottle. White gas is sold at the Glacier Bay Lodge or in Gustavus, but alcohol, butane, propane, and Sterno are not. Commercial airline safety regulations prohibit carrying flammable or explosive materials, which unfortunately includes all campstove fuels. So bring a fuel bottle for filling here, and be prepared to use only white gas.

Finding drinking water, except on islands and some ridges and high slopes, is no problem. So far, contamination has not been a problem. Glacial streams are brown with silt, but drinkable. Let the water stand overnight to settle out the silt.

Pack out everything you pack in. This includes empty cans, jars, and plastic bags and sheets. Do not bury anything but human waste, and burying it in the intertidal zone is best. In more populous areas this would not be satisfactory; here it is. Campfires are also best built in the intertidal zone where their scars will soon be erased. This is the key: try to camp without leaving a trace.

Mountain and Glacier Climbing Specialized equipment and experience are requisite to safe mountain climbing or to venturing out onto glacier ice. Check with park rangers for current information if your plans include the high peaks or glacier travel. The Fairweather Range stretches nearly 5,000 meters (16,000 feet) above sea level and scores of glaciers whiten various elevations. Spectacular climbs are assured the prepared, but you need to bring full equipment and knowledge with you. This includes rescue knowledge and gear. (See page 107 and Trips Up the Bay for logistics information. Air drops of people or supplies are prohibited.) You must know ground-to-air signals to attract attention in emergencies. Expect to be totally on your own, and make your own support-party arrangements. The terrain here is exceedingly remote. Rangers help if they can, but even making contact is unlikely in emergency situations here. (See Precautions.)

Kayaking, Canoeing, and Boating In general, kayaks are preferable to canoes in these waters. Kayaks are lighter to handle, and are less affected by wind since they ride lower in the water. This can be important. A general lack of wind may frustrate sailors here, but there's enough of it to menace paddlers. Strong gusts may blow up at any time, so stay within 500 meters (a quarter mile) of shore and at the first hint of storm, head in. The routine scheduling of city living can be a booby trap here. Setting time goals and adhering to them may interfere with your trip rather than enhance it. Don't stubbornly buck wind and waves. Don't challenge fate. Go ashore, hole up, and wait. Once you've idled back your sense of urgency to fit nature's realities, you'll find a peculiar emancipation. It's like returning to a time that predates—and transcends—the clock.

All those afloat, in no matter what type of craft, should bring lifejackets,

at least one extra paddle per craft, basic repair parts and equipment, and a Juneau tide table. Tide range approaches 8 meters (25 feet). This produces strong currents which drastically affect itinerary and timing. You can get a free ride by going with the tidal current, but be thwarted or swept back by going against it. Plan accordingly.

When ashore, carry your craft up well above the highest seaweed and barnacles, then tie the bowline to a rock or tree trunk. Do this automatically—even on an outgoing tide—and you'll never return to find your kayak or dinghy drifted off, with potential dire consequences.

Don't pursue seals, whales, or seabirds in the water. Respect seal mother-and-pup pairs hauled out on floating ice. If you panic them into diving off, they may become hopelessly separated, and the pup will die. By Federal regulation (under the Endangered Species Act) whales may not be approached closer than 500 meters (1,500 feet). This is to assure that park waters remain a protected haven for their summer feeding, but the regulation also protects you. Even without intending harm, a whale could easily capsize a kayak, canoe, or dinghy and could severely damage a larger boat.

Seawater temperatures here, even in summer, are much too cold for falling overboard. Know how to handle your craft before venturing into these waters on your own. A few kayaks may sometimes be rented in Gustavus. Guided trips are offered through a tour service there.

Yachtsmen will need the Glacier Bay chart, sold at the lodge if you don't already have one. This chart is available in 1:80,000 and 1:250,000 scales. No boating guide is available, but rangers can advise you somewhat

Many backpackers, kayakers, and day hikers get within range of backcountry destinations by catching a ride on the Thunder Bay. *You pay the regular fare plus a fee for being dropped off and picked up. Make arrangements ahead; only a few special stops can be made per trip.*

Page 118: *An angler was holding a huge silver salmon alongside the Dundas River. "Where in the world did you get that?" our photographer asked. The salmon said. . . .*

Author Ruth Kirk confirms itineraries with her charter pilot after unloading gear at Reid Glacier.

A raft party floats the Tatshenshini River in the national preserve. It joins the Alsek River, providing exciting float trip adventures.

about anchorages and courses. Extensive, specific information may be hard to come by.

Classic up-bay anchorages are Reid Inlet, Shag Cove, Blue Mouse Cove, and South Sandy Cove. Wolf Point in Lower Muir Inlet is beautiful but exposed to winds and drifting icebergs. Adams Inlet has extensive shoalwater because of glacial outwash. For additional anchorages, or for Dundas or Taylor Bay or outer-coast destinations, you will have to find someone who can pinpoint protected locations on your chart.

Inside Glacier Bay, extreme water depth, tide range, and rocky bottoms can complicate anchoring. There are no docks or mooring buoys. Icebergs may be a real threat, as well as a joy to behold (see Precautions). Beware, too, of silty deltas reaching considerable distances offshore from active glacial outwashes. Depth readings may be misleading because such submarine deposits can have an abrupt leading edge. Running aground is the only way to find them!

Prevailing winds off the ocean and Cross Sound are southwesterly. They may be fairly strong in lower Glacier Bay while upper reaches are flat calm. Intermittent winds coming off the high peaks characterize the upper bay. These are not uniform in direction, strength, or duration.

Getting drinking water is no problem, providing you have containers and a means of going ashore.

The National Park Service monitors Channel 16 daily from 8:00 a.m. to 4:00 p.m. during the summer season. Bartlett Cove park headquarters call letters are KWM-20. Outlying ranger stations at Goose Cove, Dundas Bay, Graves Harbor, or Cenotaph Island can be called directly by location name.

Rangers are here intermittently, so don't be confident of making contact. Line-of-sight is necessary for most VHF transmission, obviously a stacked deck in fjord country where high cliffs wall and seal off inlets.

Self-sufficiency is the hallmark of Glacier Bay boating. Bring all gear and supplies, including those for emergency repairs, and an extra anchor. The self-sufficiency must extend to your mind-set too. Some people are psychologically disoriented by being away from others. For them, boating here beyond Bartlett Cove may be traumatic. For wise planning, know your equipment, including your psyche.

River Float Trips Where the Tatshenshini and Alsek Rivers join, the water flow becomes triple that of the Colorado River through the Grand Canyon. This makes for one of our continent's major float trips. Together, the Tatshenshini-Alsek river corridor comprises the only break in the coast mountains from Cape Spencer to the Copper River. Several guides offer float trips under permit, strictly in summer. Write for a guide list. The trip takes a week or more. Total distance is around 200 kilometers (125 miles). High peaks, closeby glaciers, and wildlife assure superb scenery. You end up at Dry Bay, on the park's northern outer coast, where prearranged air service meets you.

Precautions

Wilderness seems wilder here than in many regions where that term is used. And some potential hazards here are rare elsewhere. *Never* travel alone. If you and your party are inexperienced, don't start out on your own here. Join a cruise or tour-boat party, or a guided kayak- or float-trip instead. Those with previous experience, however, can expect an absolute highpoint in backpacking, kayaking, or boating, or a combination of these.

About Bears Both black bears and brown/grizzly bears can be dangerous, although brown/grizzlies are more likely to be aggressive. You can't outrun either, so don't squander your energy trying. The best thing to do is to avoid a confrontation. Never go deliberately close. Use a long-focus lens for pictures. When hiking, be noisy especially when going through brush where visibility is limited. Talk, sing, whistle, or tie a jingling bell to your pack. This gives the bears fair warning, and they will usually avoid you, given that option. Stay out in open country whenever possible, especially if you've noticed bear tracks, droppings, or diggings. And avoid bear food sources such as berry patches and animal carcasses. Cook and store your food in an area well separated from where you sleep. Be scrupulously clean about your camp so odors are minimized.

Near certain trouble will result if you get between a sow and her cubs. If a bear charges you, most experts advise that you first try out-psyching it. Call in a loud but calm and authoritative voice, not a hysterical screech. The words don't matter. "Stop," and your favorite epithets are probably as good as anything.

If a bear clearly is going to attack, not just charge in bluff, your best hope of survival seems to be curling into the fetal position with your fingers clasped over the back of your neck. Unlike fighting humans, animals usually need only to exert their dominance, not to inflict prolonged punishment or to kill. If there are several of you, try linking arms and looking like a huge adversary while ordering the bear to stop. If you spot a bear, make plenty of noise and cross upwind so that it can get your scent. Surprise encounters are to be avoided if at all possible. A Bear Warning leaflet is available free at Bartlett Cove, or by mail from the superintendent. Get one and study it.

Icebergs and Glaciers Despite their beauty, floating icebergs are dangerous if approached too closely. They may turn over quickly or break up without warning. Added danger—for kayak or dinghy—comes from the waves set in motion by a rolling berg.

Enormous waves that sweep for considerable distances are set off by ice falling from tidewater glacier fronts. This is the most common danger from getting too close to a tidewater ice cliff. The National Park Service recommends staying at least a kilometer (one-half mile or more) away. The waves set up may also race along the shore, threatening kayakers or hikers who thought they were prudently removed from the glacier front. Even a grounded ice tongue, such as the Reid Glacier, may calve off enormous slabs and bergs. People have been killed in Southeastern Alaska when walking close to such ice fronts.

Venturing out onto a glacier is best left to the experienced and equipped. Ice remnants such as what is left of the Muir, Burroughs, or McBride Glaciers are a partial exception to this because they have mostly dwindled into reason-able stability. But even so, what looks like gravel may just be a thin veneer over slick ice. Last winter's snow may be hiding crevasses, great cracks like canyons, and moulins, melt holes that drop clear through the ice. If you hear the muffled roar of water, beware. The ice covering a melt stream is often thin.

Ice caves along the edge of a glacier are always dangerous. Rocks embedded in the ceiling can drop, ice slabs give way, and melt streams somewhere upslope suddenly break loose and send a torrent sluicing through a cave. Seracs—ice pinnacles—may melt out of balance and crash, a hazard both of glacier remnants and active snouts.

When Afoot Meltwater rivers are turbulent. If they come from a glacier they may be so silty that you can't see bottom. Cross such rivers with care. Keep your boots on; wet feet are better than risking a fall. Use a stout stick for balance. Unfasten your pack's bellyband so you can slip out quickly if you fall. Wide sections of river, usually the most shallow, are often the best crossing points. Angle slightly downstream as you wade. Early morning crossings are best because the lower melt rate then means shallower water.

In tidal areas or near glaciers, watch out for quickmud, sediment so newly deposited that it's still goop. The surface looks okay, but put weight on it and the deposit liquifies. Poke ahead with a staff if you have any doubt about what you're getting into. Move as quickly as possible if you feel yourself sinking in.

Hold to a compass course if you're bashing through alder thickets. You can't see out, and otherwise you may waste hours going in unhappy circles. Devil's club is an additional terror. If your necessary route leads through this thorny hell, don your sturdiest long-sleeved, long-legged clothing.

When Afloat Floating icebergs and tidewater glacier tongues are the greatest hazards afloat, as described above. If you anchor in iceberg waters, such as Reid Inlet or at Wolf Point, consider your emergency action if a large iceberg should bear down on your boat or anchor line. Know how to cut and run if your boat hook won't fend off the ice. It's better to lose an anchor and line than to contend with a big iceberg. Otherwise, don't anchor where tidal currents could bring a stream of bergs near you.

With tides ranging up to 8 meters (25 feet), you must carry dinghies and kayaks truly high on the beach when going ashore. Then secure them well by tying. Similarly, allow ample scope on the anchor line and remember that adequate water depth at high tide may be unacceptable at low tide. You'll go aground.

Firearms Warning Firearms are permitted in the undeveloped areas of the park. If you've brought one, check with a ranger. They are for emergency use only, not for display, and some types are potentially more dangerous than effective.

Nearby Attractions

Excursion Inlet An active salmon cannery operates adjacent to the ruins of a long-defunct predecessor. The massive timber frameworks of now-outlawed fish traps lie beached at the inlet's head. No tourist services are available. The inlet's western shore is in the park.

Hoonah A Tlingit Indian village, Hoonah offers motels and stores, limited dock tie-up space and fuel, scheduled flights connecting to Juneau, and charter flights anywhere. There is a public telephone, and a clinic which accepts emergency patients. A cannery in the outer harbor buys salmon and crabs from commercial fishermen.

Elfin Cove On Cross Sound, Elfin Cove is a roadless fishing village of cantilevered walkways and houses tucked along the inner reaches of a steep-sided, deep cove. A more picturesque layout is hard to imagine. Dock tie-up space generally equals demand on a first-come, first-served basis (no charge). Fuel, groceries, ice, marine supplies, and limited services are available. So are rooms, meals, liquor, hot showers, and sauna.

Juneau If you're in Juneau on a blue-sky day, consider chartering an hour's flight over the Juneau ice cap. Ask the pilot to go up the Mendenhall Glacier and come down the Taku, an advancing glacier that is actively knocking over trees, blanketing an emerald meadow, and blocking an inlet with its outwash. Tour buses run from downtown Juneau to the Mendenhall Glacier snout. This pleasant drive ends at a Forest Service visitor center with exhibits and a nature trail. Allow a half day for this trip. In downtown Juneau the State Museum offers outstanding

Skagway's historic Arctic Brotherhood Hall must have one of this nation's most intriguing facades. Here at Klondike Gold Rush National Historical Park restored structures give a picture of life in 1898 and after. Bottom photo shows, from left, Mascot Saloon, Pacific Clipper Line office, and the Boas Tailor and Furrier shop.

displays about natural history and human culture here. (Open daily in summer; no charge.) The Chamber of Commerce, on Franklin Street, provides a downtown walking tour leaflet. Highlights are St. Nicholas Russian Orthodox Church and the imposing Governor's Mansion. Juneau has been Alaska's capital since territorial days. There is a joint National Park Service-U.S. Forest Service information desk in the Federal Building lobby. Ask there for information on Admiralty Island National Monument. There are Forest Service campgrounds some distance north of Juneau. City bus service connects from the Auke Bay ferry terminal and the airport to downtown Juneau.

Haines Principal Haines area attractions include Fort William H. Seward, Sheldon Museum and Cultural Center, Alaska Indian Arts, and the Chilkat Center for the Arts, where the Chilkat Dancers perform. Along the river, north of town, bald eagles congregate in late summer and fall to feed on spawned-out salmon. There are private and state park campgrounds surrounding Haines. A road leads into the interior, joining with the Alaska Highway at Haines Junction, north of Whitehorse in Yukon Territory, Canada. Haines occupies a traditional Tlingit village site. Recent history dates from the establishment of a trading post in 1878, followed by a mission in 1881.

Skagway The Alaska Marine Highway, alias the ferry system, has its northern end at Skagway, the head of Lynn Canal. The present town was born during Klondike Gold Rush days in 1898, when 20,000 eager "stampeders" made it their staging area—and the largest Alaskan town of that day.

From Skagway, gold seekers climbed famed Chilkoot Pass, bound for Lake Bennett and a water route to the goldfields. Klondike Gold Rush National Historical Park today preserves the scene of their struggles. You can climb the same trail they did, nearly straight up via Chilkoot Pass. Scheduled bus tours operate on the new road connecting Skagway and Whitehorse. There is a National Park Service visitor center in Skagway's historic railroad depot building. The Trail of '98 Museum is inside the City Hall. A city campground and a private campground are virtually downtown. A small state park lies about 7 kilometers (4.5 miles) from the ferry terminal.

Sitka Sitka is reached by air or aboard certain state ferries and cruise ships, but not all. It was the first white settlement in Southeastern Alaska, established by Russian traders in 1799. Here Russia transferred title to Alaska into American hands following Secretary of State William H. Seward's land purchase in 1817. Today, Sitka's economy is based on a pulp mill, fishing, and a cold storage plant. Campgrounds and a range of accommodations and services are available. Points of interest include the Tlingit Cultural Center, Sheldon Jackson Museum, St. Michaels Cathedral, and Sitka National Historical Park. The park features a totem pole collection, demonstrations of native crafts, and a Russian bishop's restored house. Ask in Sitka about the new Archangel Dancers' performance schedule.

Armchair Explorations

Selected books, maps, guides, and other publications are offered for sale at the park or through the mail by the Alaska Natural History Association, Glacier Bay National Park and Preserve, Gustavus, AK 99826. Write for a free price list.

Boehm, William. *Glacier Bay*. Alaska Northwest Publishing Company.

Bohn, Dave. *Glacier Bay, The Land and the Silence*. Alaska Natural History Association.

Bohn, Dave. *Wondrous Scene*. Goose Cove Press.

Brown, Dale. *Wild Alaska*. The American Wilderness: Time-Life Books.

Brown, William E. *This Last Treasure, Alaska National Parklands*. Alaska Natural History Association.

Nautical Charts. National Oceanic and Atmospheric Administration (NOAA).

Index

☆GPO:1983—381-611/305

Handbook 123

The National Park Service expresses its appreciation to all those persons who made the preparation and production of this handbook possible.

All photography or other artwork not credited below comes from the files of Glacier Bay National Park and Preserve.

R.H. Armstrong 79 sandpiper and terns
Tom Bean 4-5, 6, 8-9, 12, 16-17, 40-41, 77, 78 puffins, 82-83, 86, 104-105, 111, 118, 119
Bruce Black 101
William Boehm 18-19, 58 moss
Belmore Browne, Courtesy of Glenbow Museum, Calgary, Alberta 98-99
Donald D. Chase 120 raft
John Cossick 42
Richard Ellis 92-95 whales
John Field 45
William O. Field, American Geographical Society 44
Gary M. Hasty 57 spruce bud
James G. Hauck 52, 57 cottonwood
W.S. Home 58 columbine
Robert Hynes 90-91
John Hopkins University, Ferdinand Hamburger, Jr. Archives 34
Mark Kelley cover
Ruth and Louis Kirk 24, 29, 36, 43, 49, 56-57, 100, 113 ship, 120 plane
Penny Knuckles 58 blueberry, 59 baneberry
David Nemeth 59 fungus
Michael J. Nigro 59 cress
Rollie Ostermick 59 skunk cabbage
Bruce Paige 10-11, 22-23, 30-31,

78 duck, 79 guillemot
Jaime Quintero 46-47
R.R. Donnelley & Sons 106, 108-109
William Rodarmore 55, 57 alder, 58 moraine
Greg Streveler 62, 79, kittiwakes, 80 top
Clarence Summers 57 spruce/hemlock
U.S. Fish and Wildlife Service 72-73 salmon, 73 eagle (Ron Singer)
Bradford Washburn 102
Manya Wik 68, 79 gulls